THE
KITCHEN DECODED

THE
KITCHEN DECODED

TOOLS, TRICKS, and RECIPES FOR GREAT FOOD

LOGAN LEVANT and **HILARY HATTENBACH**

Skyhorse Publishing

Skyhorse Publishing books may be purchased in bulk at special discounts for sales promotion, corporate gifts, fund-raising, or educational purposes. Special editions can also be created to specifications. For details, contact the Special Sales Department, Skyhorse Publishing, 307 West 36th Street, 11th Floor, New York, NY 10018 or info@skyhorsepublishing.com.

Skyhorse® and Skyhorse Publishing® are registered trademarks of Skyhorse Publishing, Inc.®, a Delaware corporation.

Visit our website at www.skyhorsepublishing.com.

10 9 8 7 6 5 4 3 2 1

Library of Congress Cataloging-in-Publication Data is available on file.

Cover and interior design by Tracy Sunrize Johnson
Cover and interior photos by Melissa Barnes
Photo styling by Alicia Buszczak

Print ISBN: 978-1-62914-695-9
Ebook ISBN: 978-1-63220-016-7

Printed in China

CONTENTS

INTRODUCTION   vii

CHAPTER 1: NITTY-GRITTY KITCHEN BASICS   1

CHAPTER 2: WHY YOU SHOULD HEART YOUR CUISINART   49

CHAPTER 3: COOKIE SHEETS—NOT JUST FOR COOKIES ANYMORE   89

CHAPTER 4: TIME FLIES WITH A MICROPLANE   115

CHAPTER 5: LE CREUSET STOCKPOT FULL OF LOVE   145

CHAPTER 6: KITCHENAID TO THE RESCUE   175

CHAPTER 7: LET'S GET THIS PARTY PLANNED!   219

ACKNOWLEDGMENTS   229

METRIC CONVERSIONS   230

INDEX   231

This book is dedicated to our moms, Alison Levant and Judith Eytel-Swar.

INTRODUCTION

As a couple of career gals on the go, we know it's tough to make time for home-cooked meals. We'd never even attempt to cook if we didn't have an arsenal of time-tested recipes and tools at our disposal to help streamline time in the kitchen. And that's why we wrote *The Kitchen Decoded*—to simplify cooking by breaking down the best tools for each task, and to provide delicious recipes that are easy to execute and quick to make.

Many people register for and purchase expensive kitchen equipment because the idea of cooking is exciting. But more often than not, the appliance ends up sitting in a cupboard, collecting dust because nobody knows how the heck to use it. *The Kitchen Decoded* takes the fear out of cooking and breaks down kitchen essentials. The chapters are organized by our favorite, tried-and-true cooking tools. A variety of manufacturers make excellent cooking equipment, but we wanted to speak from experience and give you the lowdown on the tools we use and why we chose them. The ins and outs of our featured tools are outlined in each chapter, but you do not have to own everything we recommend nor do you have to be a professional chef to make great food.

We asked a few friends to submit their favorite recipes using our book's featured tools to illustrate the many ways everyday people use the kitchen. Keep an eye out for "guest chef" recipes peppered throughout the book. We hope that you'll be inspired to put some of our tricks, tools, and recipes to work and that the outcome will be tons of yummy meals. And if you have a favorite recipe using a gadget from our book, we'd love to hear about it. Send us a message at kitchendecoded@gmail.com.

—Logan and Hilary

ABOUT US

Logan Levant began her career as a busy PR executive in the entertainment industry. Due to the long hours and high-pressure environment, she made a habit of stopping by her favorite neighborhood bakery for daily lemon-bar therapy. When the bakery owner decided to retire and take her lemon bar recipe with her, Logan had to act fast. With a passion for cooking and baking but no formal culinary training, Logan took over the bakery and set about learning everything from scratch. Armed with essential cooking tools and family recipes, she quickly transitioned from an amateur home cook to a professional chef and ran the business successfully for ten years.

During that time, whenever a friend got married, Logan gave the gift of cooking equipment hoping to encourage her friends to prepare homemade meals. After receiving several thank you notes that said, "I can't wait for you to come over and teach me how to use this," a light bulb went off and the idea for *The Kitchen Decoded* was born. Excited and inspired by a chance to teach her tricks to beginners, newlyweds, or anyone with a desire to cook, Logan closed the bakery and teamed up with Hilary to create *The Kitchen Decoded*.

Hilary Hattenbach, a children's book author and entertainment executive, has always had a passion for cooking, baking, and writing. Cofounder of the popular blog WeHeartMacandCheese.com, she has eaten enough macaroni and cheese to make a cardiologist run screaming. As an entertainment executive, she's conceived and produced award-winning, multi-platform campaigns for 20th Century Fox, Universal Pictures, DreamWorks, Disney, and Marvel. With a focus on creativity and innovation, she's instrumental in spearheading first-to-market and press worthy campaigns. In her spare time, she watches BBC mysteries with her husband, Jared, and dog, Noodle.

CHAPTER 1

NITTY-GRITTY KITCHEN BASICS

RECIPES IN THIS CHAPTER

DRY SPICE RUB	16	LEMON VINAIGRETTE	27
JERK SPICE RUB	16	BLUE CHEESE VINAIGRETTE	27
BBQ SAUCE	18	SUNDRIED TOMATO BASIL FRITTATAS	28
HONEY CHIPOTLE SAUCE	20	MASHED POTATOES	30
CHIMICHURRI SAUCE	20	TURKEY MEATBALLS	32
SOY BALSAMIC MARINADE	21	AUNT ANDREA'S RED SAUCE	34
ASIAN MARINADE	21	CHICKEN STOCK	35
MAYONNAISE	24	WHOLE ROASTED CHICKEN	36
SESAME DRESSING	25	MOM'S CHOCOLATE CHIP TOFFEE COOKIES	38
BASIL BALSAMIC DRESSING	25		
EGGLESS CAESAR DRESSING	26	BUTTERCAKE BAKERY BROWNIES	40

We know that cooking can be intimidating, especially if you watch TV shows like *Top Chef,* where contestants run around sous viding steaks and making ice cream with liquid nitrogen. Well, guess what? A lot of great cooks have never even thought about putting a steak in a vacuum-sealed bag and immersing it in water for seventy hours. Regular people don't have that kind of time or motivation. And just because something has a fancy name or looks pretty on a plate doesn't mean it tastes good. We've found that, most of the time, homey, simple meals like Mom used to make are the ones that really hit the spot. So don't panic. We won't throw any fancy cooking techniques at you. Our foolproof recipes are easy to prepare, especially with the right tools and a few tricks.

RULE #1: HAVE FUN

Cooking should be fun. It's always a challenge to try something new. But if you approach each recipe as a fresh adventure with the possibility of a delicious outcome, you're going to have a good time. Start by putting on upbeat music. Pour a glass of wine to sip, but pace yourself because you should be coherent enough to follow the recipe instructions. If you're baking or making a dish with a lot of steps, invite a friend over to help. Sometimes having a helper in the kitchen makes things go more quickly and smoothly. Think of every meal as a mini party rather than a cooking competition, and take the time to sit and enjoy the results of your hard work.

RULE #2: FOLLOW INSTRUCTIONS

Before you attempt a recipe, read it from beginning to end and make sure that you have all the necessary ingredients and equipment. Nothing creates more unneeded stress than having to run to the store for supplies. Prepare the recipe exactly as it is written. That way you will know how the chef intended it to taste. If you think it would taste better with, say, more salt or less oil, you can make a note and add your own flair next time.

RULE #3: BE WELL EQUIPPED

It isn't necessary to own every kitchen gadget ever invented. There are plenty of gimmicky gizmos and expensive, fad-inspired appliances that are borderline useless. But some tools will revolutionize the way you cook by saving time and getting results that are impossible to achieve any other way. We've identified a list of inexpensive kitchen staples that are uniquely designed to ensure accurate measuring and cooking results. Take some time to review the guide below to get a handle on your kitchen's most crucial tools. Don't feel pressured to run out and buy everything on the list. Once you know the recipes you'd like to try, consider which tools might make the job easier.

RECIPE LEGEND

All of the recipes in *The Kitchen Decoded* are marked with the letters GF, DF, and V, where appropriate, to indicate Gluten-Free, Dairy-Free (might still contain eggs), and Vegetarian.

TOOLS

1. CUTTING BOARD: A good cutting board should have a large surface and be made of a thick, indestructible material. Wood is preferable, as it won't damage knives. Use baking soda or lemon juice to sterilize the board after use. Prices range from $10–$50.

2. KITCHEN SHEARS: A sturdy pair of stainless steel kitchen shears is a must-have for cutting poultry, snipping herbs and flower stems, hacking a lemon from a tree, opening bags of food, or shaping parchment to fit baking pans. You'll be surprised how often you reach for them. Prices range from $8–$100, if you're feeling fancy.

3. CHEF'S KNIFE: An 8- or 9-inch stainless steel chef's knife is ideal for most of your chopping needs. Do not store your knives in drawers—that will dull the blade. Attach them to a magnet on the wall or store in a knife block to keep the blades from getting damaged. You don't need a professional chef's knife, which can cost hundreds of dollars. A perfectly good chef's knife can be purchased for $20 and up.

4. PARING KNIFE: A paring knife measure between $2\frac{1}{2}$ and 4 inches long and is great for smaller peeling, coring, and slicing jobs. Prices often start at $12.

5. SERRATED KNIFE: A serrated knife measures between 6 and 10 inches and has grooves in the blade. Excellent for cutting through bread crust and slicing without squishing the loaf. Prices range from $15 and up.

6. MEASURING CUP SET: For the most accurate quantities, dry ingredients should only be measured in a graduated set of cups that includes $\frac{1}{4}$ cup, $\frac{1}{3}$ cup, $\frac{1}{2}$ cup, and 1 cup. Fill the cups to the brim and level them off with back of a knife. Prices range from $3–$35 depending on style.

7. GLASS MEASURING CUP: Liquids should only be measured in a glass, heat-resistant cup with a spout for easy pouring. We recommend a 2-cup measuring cup. You'll find a million uses for this little kitchen helper. Perfect for mixing up dressings, warming up liquids in the microwave, catching juice from the citrus juicer, and much more. A 2-cup measure ranges from $5–$12.

8. MEAT THERMOMETER: Essential for checking the temperature of meat and testing for doneness, it measures temperatures as high as 220°F. Prices range from $7–$30.

9. CANDY THERMOMETER: Great for making candy, checking the temperature of caramel, or if you never make candy, it's helpful to monitor oil temperatures for frying. Measures temperatures up to 400°F. Prices range from $6–$30.

10. MEASURING SPOONS: These are used to measure smaller amounts of liquids and dry ingredients. Sold as a graduated set that includes $\frac{1}{4}$ teaspoon, $\frac{1}{2}$ teaspoon, 1 teaspoon, and 1 tablespoon. Prices range from $1–$20.

11. OVEN THERMOMETER: An oven often has a mind of its own and may cook food at whatever temperature it pleases. That's why an oven thermometer is a lifesaver in the kitchen. It hangs on a rack in the oven and measures the heat in the oven. By checking the thermometer, you can adjust the temperature up or down depending on whether your oven runs hot or cool. Prices range from $2–$20.

12. ICE CREAM SCOOPS: While these guys do a bang up job of scooping up your favorite frozen dessert, they are also extra handy for scooping up balls of dough to create even portions for cookies, cupcakes, muffins, scones, biscuits, and more. Look for scoops with a trigger handle that uses spring action to release the food. Available in a few different sizes, we use a 2-ounce scoop for Buttercake Bakery Chocolate Cake/Cupcakes (pages 192-4), and a 2-ounce scoop for the Donut Holes (page 172). Heck, we even use them for Turkey Meatballs (page 32), Sundried Basil Tomato Frittatas (page 28), and Veggie Fritters (pages 75-76). Prices range from $7–$25.

1

2

3

4

5

6

2

7

8

6

1. **TONGS:** Instead of using your hands or forks to extract ingredients from hot pans and toss food on the grill, tongs keep you an arm's length from the heat. Prices range from $5-$20.

2. **WOODEN SPOONS:** These versatile spoons do not conduct heat, nor will they scratch and damage your metal pots and pans. Have a variety on hand to tackle different jobs from stirring batters to sautéing proteins, starches, and vegetables. Prices range from under $1-$20 depending on quality of the wood.

3. **METAL WHISK:** Made of looped wire, a whisk is what you need to whip ingredients by hand. A small one is perfect for whipping up dressings or scrambled eggs and easily fits inside a glass measuring cup. A larger whisk is great for combining dry ingredients by hand. Prices range from $2-$25.

4. **HEAT PROOF SPATULA:** Silicone spatulas are heat-resistant and can be dipped in melted chocolate with reckless abandon. They are a must-have for scraping down the sides of your stand mixer to incorporate all the ingredients and get every last bit of batter out of the bowl into your baking pan. Prices range from $2-$15.

5. **ROLLING PIN:** A heavy wooden rolling pin will roll out large pieces of dough with the most efficiency. They aren't expensive and they will ensure an even thickness on crusts and baked goods. It can also be used as a meat tenderizer to flatten meat for more even cooking. Prices range from $6-$20.

6. **MIXING BOWLS:** It's helpful to have a set of three or four mixing bowls. Many are sold Russian nesting doll style, where the smaller ones fit inside the larger ones. Glass and metal bowls are versatile and can easily be turned into double boilers. Porcelain bowls work well too and can moonlight as serving bowls. Prices range from $15-$60.

7. **SLOTTED SPOON:** Use slotted spoons to lift food out of hot liquid, allowing excess water or oil to pass through the holes. Perfect for blanching or lifting fritters and donuts out of oil. Find one that is heat resistant. Prices range from under $1-$20.

8. **OVEN MITT:** We recommend a long glove style mitt to protect your hand and forearm from burns when pulling hot pans from the oven or stovetop. Prices range from $6-$25.

1. CAN OPENER: Invest in a decent hand-held can opener and you won't have to struggle with lids in the middle of a recipe. Prices range from $4-$25.

2. MANDOLINE: These extra-sharp slicers come with straight and wavy blades and create even slices in a range of thicknesses. Perfect for making Cora's Sliced Sweet Pickles (page 150), citrus slices for our Velvet Hammer Sangria (page 142), or julienned Baked Sweet Potato Fries (page 106). Sold with a large food holder to protect your fingers, the mandoline sits on the counter while you run the intended ingredient across the blade. It's a good idea to also buy a safety glove to wear while slicing, because those blades are insanely sharp. Prices range from $10-$100.

3. COOLING RACK: These woven metal racks allow air to flow under and around hot pans. Use them to cool cookie sheets and cake pans when they come out of the oven. Place one inside a cookie sheet and you've got an instant roasting pan. This is also great for draining fried foods. Prices range from $5-$25.

4. MESH COLANDER: Whether it's to drain beans for Black Bean Patties (page 78), sift flour, or shake powdered sugar on Buttercake Bakery Lemon Bars (pages 134–36), a mesh colander is a workhorse in the kitchen. Get a few in different sizes. We like to use a tiny one (or a sieve) to strain citrus and catch the seeds and a large one to drain pasta. Prices range from $2-$20.

5. KITCHEN TIMER: Keeping track of your baking and cooking times is crucial to good results. Pick up a portable kitchen timer that can move around the kitchen with you and time the different steps in the recipe. Never burn those cookies again! Prices range from $4-$40.

6. GARLIC PRESS: No time or patience to mince that garlic? Garlic presses squeeze the cloves through tiny holes and abracadabra!—instant minced garlic. Prices range from $3-$15.

7. CITRUS JUICERS: We're citrus maniacs, and we'd be lost without a decent citrus juicer. Press (7a) or reamer (7b), you'll get way more juice out of citrus fruits with these tools than squeezing by hand. For large quantities of fresh juice, consider investing in an electric juicer. Prices range from $6-over $100.

8. PEELER: Spend a little extra money on a sturdy vegetable peeler and it'll make quick work of carrot, apple, and potato peels. Prices range from $2-$20.

9. FUNNEL: To avoid big messes, use small and large funnels to transfer dressings, gravies, dry rubs, oil, and juice into bottles. Prices range from $1-$25.

1. BUNDT CAKE PAN: A ring shaped metal pan with fluted sides and tube in the center that creates the signature hole in the center of the bundt cake. The shape allows more of the batter to touch the surface of the pan, which makes for quicker bake times and more even heat distribution. Some bundt cake pans come with patterns etched into the metal in case you want your cake to look a bit fancier. Prices range from $10–$30.

2. CAKE PAN: Have at least one set of round cake pans with a 2-inch rim on hand, because you never know when you'll be inspired to make a double layer cake. Most cake recipes call for a 9-inch set. But they do range in size from 3 inches to 16 inches. Prices range from $10–$25.

3. LOAF PAN: Measuring 9 x 5 x 4-inch and 8½ x 4½ x 2½-inch, loaf pans are used for loaf cakes like our Buttercake Bakery Banana Cake (pages 187–88), or even meatloaf. Stainless steel with a nonstick coating works great for all uses. Prices range from $5–$20.

4. SPRINGFORM CAKE PAN: A springform is an anodized aluminum or stainless steel cake pan with removable sides. It's important to use this pan when preparing the Buttercake Bakery Cheesecake (pages 210–12), Citrus Almond Cake (pages 204–6), or any delicate baked good so as not to damage the cake when taking it out of the pan. Prices range from $10–$25.

5. PIE PAN: Pie pans range in size from 8–10 inches and are fashioned out of stainless steel, aluminum, or glass. We like glass because it's nonreactive and clear so you can see the doneness of the crust for pies and quiches. Prices range from $10–$25.

6. CUPCAKE/MUFFIN TIN: These pans typically yield 12 muffins or cupcakes and can hold about a ½ cup batter in each slot. Line them with cupcake papers to add a decorative touch and make for a quick and easy cleanup. Use a 2-ounce ice cream scoop to measure out batter, and it fills the slots perfectly. Prices range from $7–$20.

7. METAL BROWNIE PAN: A 12½ x 9-inch pan in anodized aluminum is perfect for cooking Buttercake Bakery Brownies (page 40) and Buttercake Bakery Lemon Bars (page 134–36) as well as other dense cakes and casseroles. Prices range from $16–$20.

8. GLASS LASAGNA TRAY (3-INCH EDGE): A 9 x 13 x 3-inch glass baking pan is a kitchen staple for lasagnas and casseroles but also essential for gratins and roasting vegetables. Prices range from $12–$30.

1. SAUTÉ PAN/SKILLET: A set of skillets or sauté pans made of clad stainless steel with a nonstick coating are essential if you plan to do a lot of cooking. Available in a range of sizes and depths, look for pans with lids for steaming, sautéing, and browning. Avoid using metal utensils in these pans, because they will scratch the surface. A nice set ranges in price from $100–$500.

2. BAKING PARCHMENT: This paper, sold in rolls next to the aluminum foil and plastic wrap in grocery aisles, makes a great disposable nonstick surface for baking. Line cookie sheets and cake pans so the food will slide right off. And it makes cleaning up a snap. Prices range from $4–$11.

3. PASTRY BRUSH: It's great to have a few of these in your arsenal of cooking tools for brushing oils and marinades on vegetables and meats. Prices range from $2–$15.

4. RESEALABLE BAG: Not just for leftovers, these bags are great for marinating proteins, coating foods with spices, and freezing. Pick a brand that is freezer safe. Prices range from $4–$12.

5. NONSTICK COOKING SPRAY: This canned oil is sprayed on cookware as a light coating to help keep ingredients from sticking. It also saves a few calories if you don't want to use butter or olive oil on every cooking surface. Prices range from $3–$8.

6. SILICONE BAKING MAT: If you purchase one of these, you'll never need to buy another roll of parchment paper. They are heat resistant up to 580°F. A great investment to prevent food from sticking to cookie sheets and to streamline cleanup. Prices range from $8–$35.

7. SMALL (2- OR 3-QUART) SAUCEPOT: Make sure to invest in a good quality saucepot with a fitted lid made out of clad stainless steel that is nonreactive and won't easily burn. This pot is great for cooking sauces, rice, and oatmeal. Prices range from $20–$150.

8. PLASTIC WRAP: Package up leftovers in plastic wrap before storing in the refrigerator or freezer. You can also use it to line measuring cups before measuring sticky ingredients—yank it out and the ingredients will slide off the wrap. Price ranges from $3–$11.

9. ALUMINUM FOIL: Also known as tin foil, these sheets are excellent for wrapping up foods, keeping baked veggies and meats from sticking to surfaces, and covering pans to catch drips from casseroles and cobblers to expedite cleanup. Prices range from $2–$6 for non-industrial packages.

FOOD PREP TRICKS

Here are a few tricks to help you speed through your recipe prep work.

INGREDIENT CHECKLIST: The French phrase *"mise en place"* means "together in place." This is how great chefs stay organized in the kitchen. Before you begin, take out all the necessary ingredients for your recipe, and don't just eyeball quantities. Chop, slice, and measure everything first to make sure you have enough, and this will ensure that the cooking process goes smoothly.

ASSEMBLE YOUR EQUIPMENT: Place all required attachments and tools needed for the recipe on the counter before you start cooking. You don't want to fumble through drawers and cupboards mid-recipe.

ALWAYS USE SHARP KNIVES: Not only is it safer, it's much more efficient and allows you to slice evenly.

STABILIZE CUTTING BOARDS: Put a dishtowel or damp paper towel under your cutting board to keep it from sliding around while you prep.

CLEAN AS YOU GO: Toss out scraps and empty containers once steps are complete. Put away ingredients after use. While food bakes in the oven, clear and wipe the counters and rinse off equipment. All of this will cut way down on cleanup time after the meal when all you want to do is relax.

USING GARLIC: Fresher = sweeter. The best garlic has a firm exterior and should not be bruised, sprouted, soft, or shriveled. Cloves with green shoots should be tossed, as they add bitterness to food. Always peel garlic unless the recipe specifies otherwise. To get the skin off easily, press your palm down on the flat side of a chef's knife (please, not the sharp edge!) or use the bottom of a can and bang it on the garlic clove to loosen the skin. Cut off the tough stem end with a knife. Use your microplane, garlic press, or chef's knife to mince garlic.

CUTTING ONIONS: To dice an onion, start by cutting off the top end. Next, slice the onion in half through the root and peel off the skin. Make a series of small vertical slices through the onion. Turn the onion and make horizontal slices across until you have small diced pieces. More slices will create a finer dice. For half-moon slices, cut the onion in half from stem end to root end. Peel the skin and place the flat side facing down and cut vertical slices until you have even half moon shapes.

JUICING CITRUS: We love citrus and a lot of recipes in this book call for lemons, limes, and oranges. For optimal juicing, the citrus should be room temperature. To maximize juice output, roll the fruit on the counter under your palm to soften them up before you cut them open. Use a citrus juice press to squeeze out the juice, or use a fork to pierce the inside of the fruit to break open the segments before squeezing by hand. Run a zester/grater over the fruit skin to zest before you juice. Only run the zester in one direction or the teeth will dull. Instead of grating zest into a separate container or onto parchment paper, hold the zester over the mixing bowl and zest directly into the mix. The aromatic citrus oils that are released into the bowl will give the dish a zingy finish.

AVOCADO: To remove the pit easily, knock the sharp edge of a knife against the pit until it sticks and twist to loosen and remove. Not using the whole thing? Leave the pit in the remaining avocado to prevent browning and run a cut piece of lemon or lime around the exposed fruit, then wrap tightly with plastic wrap.

DRY VS. FRESH HERBS: Dried herbs can be substituted for fresh herbs but it's not a one to one conversion. 1 teaspoon dried =1 tablespoon fresh. This works best with oregano, thyme, sage, and rosemary. Try to use fresh herbs when your recipe calls for basil, mint, or parsley to get the most flavor into your dish.

SEPARATING EGGS: Crack an egg in half. Working over a bowl, pass the yolk back and forth between the two half-shells until all of the egg white falls into the bowl. The remaining yolk in one of the half-shells can be placed in a separate bowl if using, or tossed out. If you drop a shell into your bowl, use one half of an empty eggshell to scoop it out.

MEASURING STICKY INGREDIENTS: Avoid a sticky mess and spray measuring cups with a nonstick cooking spray before measuring honey, molasses, or peanut butter. The contents will slide right out and into your bowl.

BOILING WATER: Cover the pot when boiling water, and it'll be noodle-ready much quicker.

GLUTEN-FREE SOY SAUCE: Soy sauce contains a small amount of gluten. For a gluten-free alternative, look for gluten-free soy sauce at the supermarket.

RUBS AND MARINADES

These marinades, rubs, and dipping sauces jazz up meals in a jiffy.

RUBS

Rubs made of spice and herb combinations with a little salt and sugar can be applied to meat, fish, or poultry right before cooking for added flavor. Rubs will keep for up to six months in an airtight container.

DRY SPICE RUB

(GF, DF, V)

1 tablespoon salt

1½ tablespoons packed brown sugar

1 tablespoon paprika

2 teaspoons garlic powder

2 teaspoons dried mustard

1½ teaspoons pepper

½ teaspoon ground coriander

½ teaspoon ground cumin

½ teaspoon dried thyme

½ teaspoon red chili flakes

1 teaspoon chili powder

Combine all ingredients in an airtight container with a lid and shake to mix. Sprinkle rub on protein, 1 teaspoon rub to every ¾ pound of protein.

JERK SPICE RUB

(GF, DF, V)

1 tablespoon packed brown sugar

2 teaspoons ground allspice

1 teaspoon dried thyme

½ teaspoon ground cinnamon

½ teaspoon ground cumin

½ teaspoon ground ginger

½ teaspoon paprika

½ teaspoon salt

½ teaspoon pepper

¼ teaspoon grated nutmeg

¼–½ teaspoon cayenne (depending on your heat preference)

Combine all ingredients in an airtight container. When ready to use, combine jerk rub with 2 tablespoons olive oil in resealable plastic bag with 2 pounds of protein. Marinate in the refrigerator for 30 minutes–2 hours. Tastes great on chicken, pork, or shrimp.

MARINADES

These marinades infuse a burst of flavor into everything they touch. You can even reserve a portion to be used as a dipping sauce. Try them on fish, poultry, beef, pork, and tofu. All marinades accommodate 2 pounds of meat. Fish shouldn't marinate more than 1 hour in the fridge. All other proteins can marinate up to 4 hours in the fridge. Marinades can be made a day ahead of time.

BBQ SAUCE

(GF, DF)

1 tablespoon extra-virgin olive oil

2 cloves garlic, minced

¾ cup ketchup

2 tablespoons cider vinegar

2 tablespoons packed brown sugar

2 teaspoons soy sauce

2 teaspoons lemon juice

1 teaspoon Dijon mustard

½ teaspoon sriracha (found in the international aisle of your market)

½ teaspoon Worcestershire sauce

1½ teaspoons Dry Spice Rub (page 16)

1. In a medium sauté pan on medium low heat, add the oil and garlic. Sauté until fragrant, about 2 minutes.

2. Reduce heat to low, add in the rest of the ingredients, and simmer for 15 minutes.

3. Brush BBQ Sauce (warm or chilled) on meats during the last 10 minutes of cooking or grilling. It will keep for 5 days in an airtight container in the fridge.

HONEY CHIPOTLE SAUCE

(GF, DF, V)

¼ cup honey

2 tablespoons extra-virgin olive oil

3 chipotle peppers in adobo (found in the international aisle of your market)

2 tablespoons balsamic vinegar

2 tablespoons Dijon mustard

1 clove garlic, chopped

juice from 4 limes

1 teaspoon ground cumin

¼ cup cilantro, roughly chopped

¼ teaspoon salt

¼ teaspoon pepper

In a food processor, combine all ingredients until pureed. Can be used as a marinade or dipping sauce. If using as a marinade, place in a resealable plastic bag with protein or veggies and refrigerate. Follow the marinating guidelines above.

TRICK

Cilantro stems aren't bitter like parsley stems—the stem flavor actually packs a bit more of punch. Feel free to toss in the stems too and waste less!

CHIMICHURRI SAUCE

(GF, DF, V)

2 cups parsley leaves

½ cup cilantro leaves

1 clove garlic

1 cup vegetable or canola oil

½ cup distilled white vinegar

2 tablespoons sambal oelek (Indonesian chili garlic paste found in the international aisle of your market)

1 tablespoon lemon juice

1 tablespoon fresh oregano (or 1 teaspoon dried)

1 teaspoon granulated sugar

salt and pepper to taste

In a food processor, add all ingredients and blend for 30 seconds until well combined.

Can be made ahead of time and stored for up to 5 days in an airtight container in the fridge. Use as a marinade or dipping sauce. If using as marinade, place in a resealable plastic bag with protein or veggies and refrigerate. Follow the marinating guidelines above.

SOY BALSAMIC MARINADE

(DF, V)

¼ cup soy sauce

¼ cup balsamic vinegar

⅓ cup extra-virgin olive oil

1 tablespoon Dijon mustard

2 teaspoons packed brown sugar

2 cloves garlic, roughly chopped

2 teaspoons fresh rosemary, chopped

salt and pepper to taste

Combine all ingredients in a resealable plastic bag and shake to mix ingredients together. If using as a marinade, place in a resealable plastic bag with protein or veggies and refrigerate. Follow the marinating guidelines above.

ASIAN MARINADE

(DF, V)

½ cup soy sauce

½ cup seasoned rice vinegar

1-inch piece of ginger, roughly chopped

3 cloves garlic, roughly chopped

3 scallions, chopped

zest from 1 orange

2 tablespoons packed brown sugar

2 tablespoons extra-virgin olive oil

1 teaspoon pepper

½ teaspoon salt

Combine all ingredients in a resealable plastic bag. Shake to mix ingredients together and add protein or veggies to the bag, reseal, and refrigerate. Follow the marinating guidelines above.

DRESSINGS

Tired of eating the same old salad every night? Spruce up greens with these quick and yummy dressings. All the dressings are made with less oil, salt, and sugar than the store-bought varieties. They can be stored in the refrigerator for up to a week. Bring dressing to room temperature 30 minutes before you serve.

1. Mayonnaise, 2. Sesame Dressing, 3. Eggless Caesar Dressing

4. **Basil Balsamic Dressing,** 5. **Lemon Vinaigrette,** 6. **Blue Cheese Vinaigrette**

MAYONNAISE

(GF, V)

1 egg yolk, room temperature

½ teaspoon salt

1 teaspoon Dijon mustard

¼ teaspoon granulated sugar

2 teaspoons lemon juice

1 tablespoon distilled white vinegar

1 cup canola oil

1. In a food processor, add the yolk, salt, mustard, sugar, lemon juice, and vinegar. Blend for 30 seconds.

2. With the motor running, SLOWLY pour droplets of canola oil through the small feed tube. Wait a few seconds between additions. As the mixture starts to thicken, add the remainder of the oil in a thin steady stream. This process should take about 2 minutes to add all the oil.

Serving Suggestion: Spread on sandwiches or use to make chicken salad, potato salad, egg salad, or creamy dresssings.

Homemade mayo will last 3 days.

TRICK

Use fresh eggs for mayo. To test freshness, put the egg in a small bowl of water. If the egg sinks, it's fresh, and if it floats to the top and stands on one end, it's not.

SESAME DRESSING

(DF, V)

⅔ cup canola oil

⅓ cup rice wine vinegar

1½ tablespoons soy sauce

1½ teaspoons toasted sesame oil

1½ teaspoons mustard powder

1 teaspoon ground ginger

4 teaspoons packed brown sugar

1 tablespoon sesame seeds

Combine all ingredients in a container with a lid and shake until the ingredients are well blended.

Serving Suggestion: Pour on top of shredded cabbage, green onions, carrots, bell peppers, and snow peas.

BASIL BALSAMIC DRESSING

(GF, DF, V)

¼ cup balsamic vinegar

1 tablespoon Dijon mustard

1 teaspoon honey

1 clove garlic, grated

½ teaspoon salt

½ teaspoon pepper

⅓ cup extra-virgin olive oil

2 tablespoons fresh basil, chopped

Combine all ingredients in a container with a lid and shake until well blended.

Serving Suggestion: Toss with spring lettuce mix and tomatoes, cucumber, and avocado.

EGGLESS CAESAR DRESSING

(GF)

3 cloves garlic

6 oil-packed anchovy fillets, chopped

1 tablespoon Dijon mustard

1 tablespoon white vinegar

juice from ½ a lemon

¼ cup grated Parmesan cheese

¼ teaspoon Worcestershire sauce

a dash hot sauce

¼ teaspoon pepper

¼ teaspoon salt

½ cup extra-virgin olive oil

1. In a food processor, add the garlic and anchovies and pulse 10 times until turned into small chunks.

2. Add Dijon mustard, white vinegar, lemon juice, Parmesan cheese, Worcestershire sauce, hot sauce, pepper, and salt and pulse until combined.

3. With the food processor switched to ON, slowly add the extra-virgin olive oil through the small feed tube.

Serving Suggestion: Toss with romaine hearts, croutons, and extra Parmesan cheese.

LEMON VINAIGRETTE

(GF, DF, V)

½ cup extra-virgin olive oil

zest from 1 lemon plus ⅓ cup lemon juice

1 tablespoon shallot, minced

1 tablespoon Dijon mustard

2 teaspoons honey

salt and pepper to taste

Combine all ingredients in a container with a lid and shake until well mixed.

Serving Suggestion: Toss with arugula and Parmesan cheese.

BLUE CHEESE VINAIGRETTE

(GF, V)

1 clove garlic

½ cup blue cheese crumbles

3 tablespoons cider vinegar

1 teaspoon Dijon mustard

1 teaspoon granulated sugar

½ teaspoon salt

½ teaspoon pepper

¼ cup extra-virgin olive oil

Add all ingredients to a food processor and blend until combined.

Serving Suggestion: Toss with iceberg lettuce, tomatoes, and bacon.

SUNDRIED TOMATO BASIL FRITTATAS

(GF, V)

Love quiche but hate the hassle of making a crust? These quickie breakfast frittatas are for you. Make them with any combination of flavors. Try ham and gruyere, broccoli and cheddar, or bacon and spinach.

8 large eggs

¼ cup whole milk

¼ cup basil, chopped

¼ cup goat cheese, crumbled

½ cup Parmesan, grated

⅓ sundried tomatoes in oil, chopped

¼ teaspoon salt

¼ teaspoon pepper

1. Preheat oven to 350°F. Spray a muffin tin with nonstick cooking spray.

2. In a bowl, whisk together all ingredients.

3. Use an ice cream scoop to divide the egg mixture among the prepared muffin tin.

4. Bake for 10–12 minutes until the eggs are set. Serve warm.

MASHED POTATOES

(GF, V)

Holiday dinners just aren't complete without a big, buttery dish of mashed potatoes. We add half-and-half to make these potatoes extra rich and creamy.

2 pounds yukon gold potatoes, peeled and chopped into 1-inch cubes

1 teaspoon + ½ teaspoon salt, divided

¾ cup half-and-half

2 cloves garlic

4 tablespoons (2-ounces) unsalted butter, room temperature

½ teaspoon pepper

chives (optional for serving)

1. Place the potatoes in a stockpot with cold water and 1 teaspoon salt. Turn on the heat to medium and bring to a boil, then reduce heat to low and simmer for 15–20 minutes.

2. Cook the potatoes until a knife can be inserted and pushed through with no resistance.

3. While the potatoes cook, in a separate pot, combine the half-and-half, garlic, and butter.

4. Cook on low heat until the butter melts and the mixture is warm. Remove and dispose of the garlic.

5. Drain cooked potatoes in a colander. Return the potatoes to the hot stockpot for 1 minute and allow any excess moisture to evaporate.

6. Transfer potatoes to a stand mixer. On low speed (speed 2) slowly add the warm milk mixture and combine just until lumps disappear. **Do not overmix or the potatoes will become gummy.** Season with salt and pepper. Transfer to a serving dish and serve warm. Top with chives if using.

TURKEY MEATBALLS

Turkey meatballs get a bad rap for being bland. These are anything but. Using a food processor reduces prep time and helps distribute the flavor evenly. We bake the meatballs instead of frying them to reduce calories and cleanup time.

¼ cup chicken stock

6 cloves garlic

1 small onion, cut into large chunks

2 tablespoons fresh parsley

1 tablespoon fresh thyme

1 teaspoon fresh rosemary

¼ teaspoon red pepper flakes

1 package (20-ounces) ground turkey

1 egg, beaten

¼ cup grated Parmesan cheese

⅓ cup panko breadcrumbs (Japanese-style flakey breadcrumbs)

1 teaspoon salt

¾ teaspoon pepper

1. Preheat oven to 350°F. Line a cookie sheet with tin foil and lightly coat with nonstick cooking spray.

2. In a food processor, add chicken stock, garlic, onion, parsley, thyme, rosemary, and red pepper flakes. Pulse 30 times to create a puree.

3. In a large mixing bowl, use a rubber spatula to gently combine turkey, egg, Parmesan cheese, panko breadcrumbs, and the herb mixture from step 2. Do not overmix or the meatballs will be tough.

4. Use an ice cream scoop to scoop the turkey mixture onto the prepared cookie sheet (they should be the size of golf balls.) Place the balls 1 inch apart.

5. Bake for 15 minutes, then use tongs to flip each meatball and bake for an additional 5 minutes.

TRICK

Meatballs can be made ahead of time and frozen in airtight container or freezer bag. Defrost later and serve with spaghetti and Aunt Andrea's Red Sauce (page 34).

AUNT ANDREA'S RED SAUCE

(GF)

This recipe was contributed by guest chef Tony Lipp.

"My aunt, Andrea Thais, made this for me about fifteen years ago, and it was one of those sauces that you literally licked off the plate after you were out of pasta. While the recipe itself bears little resemblance to any of the classic Italian red sauces, it manages to impress even the staunchest of purists. Where did she find it? If memory serves, it was given to her by a friend from one of those gorgeous yet very cold countries, like Sweden or Denmark. I have tinkered with it (only mildly) over the years and present to you the following recipe. It pleases—and occasionally thrills—a crowd every time, without fail. The substantial quantity of slowly cooked garlic combined with the umami lusciousness of the anchovy paste really bring this sauce together." —TONY LIPP

1 can (14.5 ounces) diced tomatoes

1 can (14.5 ounces) crushed tomatoes

½ cup extra-virgin olive oil, divided in half

12 whole garlic cloves, peeled

2 tablespoons anchovy paste

kosher salt to taste

red pepper flakes to taste

1 tablespoon butter

½–1 cup fresh basil leaves, roughly chopped

TRICK

To remove multiple cloves of garlic from their skin, place the cloves inside a metal bowl and cover the bowl with another similar sized metal bowl. Holding tight, shake the bowls like crazy and within seconds the skins will fly off the garlic like magic.

1. In a stockpot over low heat, cook the diced tomatoes, crushed tomatoes, olive oil, garlic, and anchovy paste. Simmer (small bubbles will form around the edges of the pot) for 1 hour.

2. After the first hour, use a slotted spoon to fish out the garlic cloves from the sauce. Crush each clove in a garlic press and mince the garlic into a paste, then add it back into the simmering tomato sauce.

3. Add ¼ cup olive oil, and continue cooking on low heat for 25 minutes.

4. Add salt (to taste), red chili pepper flakes (to taste), and butter, and cook for an additional 20 minutes.

5. Remove pot from the flame just before serving. Add fresh basil leaves.

CHICKEN STOCK

(GF)

This is easy to make and has a far superior flavor to the canned or boxed stuff, though we suggest always having some on hand just in case.

1 whole chicken (about 4 pounds)

1 yellow onion, cut in large chunks

2 carrots, coarsely chopped

2 stalks of celery, coarsely chopped

1 head garlic, unpeeled, cut crosswise

2 bay leaves

6 sprigs fresh parsley

6 sprigs fresh thyme

1 teaspoon salt

1 teaspoon whole black peppercorns

water, enough to cover the ingredients in the pot

1. Place all ingredients in stockpot and bring to a boil over medium-high heat, then reduce heat and simmer uncovered for 1½ hours.

2. Remove from heat and pour stock through a mesh colander into a large bowl to catch the liquid. Discard solids. Chill the stock overnight; the fat will rise to the top and solidify. Remove and discard the layer of fat before use. Store in the fridge for up to 5 days. If not using right away, freeze the stock for up to 3 months. You can freeze small portions in an ice cube tray or pour into a freezer bag and freeze flat. Once frozen, stand it up and store on its side.

WHOLE ROASTED CHICKEN

(GF)

Want to impress your friends and family with an elegant and delicious one-pot meal that won't break the bank? This Whole Roasted Chicken is just the ticket. The flavor of the bird is enhanced by adding a compound butter mixture of lemon juice, zest, and fresh herbs to the skin just prior to baking. While the chicken roasts, its juices flavor the veggies underneath. It's simple to make, and because there's only one pot, cleanup is a snap.

CHICKEN

1 broiler/fryer chicken (3-4 pounds), giblets discarded, room temperature

salt and pepper

½ batch (2 ounces) Herb Butter (page 72), room temperature

2 tablespoons extra-virgin olive oil

1 lemon, cut in quarters

1 yellow onion, cut in quarters

VEGGIES

2 tablespoons extra-virgin olive oil

3 cloves garlic, roughly chopped

2 yellow onions, cut into ½-inch half-rounds

4 carrots, peeled and cut in chunks

2 potatoes, peeled and cut into 1-inch dice

TRICK

No need for a roasting rack, the veggies act as one.

1. Preheat oven to 375°F.

2. Pat the chicken dry with paper towels. Sprinkle salt and pepper on the inside and outside of the chicken to season it.

3. In a small bowl, mix herb compound butter with 2 tablespoons olive oil and set aside.

4. Place the lemon pieces and onion in the cavity of the chicken. Use your fingers to rub the butter and oil mixture all over the outside of the chicken, and set aside.

5. In a large mixing bowl, toss all of the ingredients for the veggies together. Transfer vegetable mixture to the stockpot. Place the seasoned chicken, breast side up on top of the veggies.

6. Place the stockpot in the oven uncovered and roast the chicken for 1¼–1¾ hours, rotating the pan once halfway through cooking time. Roast until the breast temperature registers 160°F and the thigh 175°F on a meat thermometer.

7. Remove from oven, transfer to a cutting board, and tent the chicken with tin foil for 10 minutes before carving. Add veggies to the serving platter with cut chicken and serve warm.

MOM'S CHOCOLATE CHIP TOFFEE COOKIES

(v)

"These cookies are chewy and delicious. I can't think of a party when these have not been on my mom's menu. I'm not a fan of nuts in cookies, so the toffee provides a nice crunch." —LOGAN

2 cups all-purpose flour

1 teaspoon baking soda

1 teaspoon salt

2 sticks (8 ounces) unsalted butter, room temperature

¾ cup granulated sugar

¾ cup packed brown sugar

2 eggs, room temperature

1 teaspoon pure vanilla extract

1 bag (12 ounces) semisweet chocolate chips

1 bag (8 ounces) English toffee bits (such as Heath)

TRICK

Turn these cookies into ice cream sandwiches. Add a scoop of your favorite ice cream to the middle of one cookie, place another on top, and press down. You can make these ahead of time. Wrap each one in plastic wrap and freeze until ready to serve.

1. Preheat oven to 375°F. Line 3 pans with parchment or silicone baking mats.

2. In a small mixing bowl, combine the flour, salt, and baking soda.

3. In a stand mixer, cream the butter, brown sugar, and granulated sugar on low (speed 2) and gradually increase speed to medium (speed 4) until mixture is pale and fluffy, about 5 minutes.

4. Add eggs one at a time, mixing on low (speed 2) after each addition, followed by the vanilla. Scrape down the sides of the bowl and beater with a spatula to make sure everything is well combined.

5. Add flour mixture in small batches on low (speed 2.) Scrape down the sides of the bowl with a spatula after the addition. Switch OFF machine.

6. Add the chips and toffee and turn ON the mixer to the STIR setting. Run until just combined.

7. Use a 2-ounce ice cream scoop and place 12 balls of dough on each tray. Use your hand to flatten down the dough slightly.

8. Bake for 10–12 minutes, until golden brown, turning the tray once during baking. Let cookies cool on sheet for 2 minutes and transfer to cooling rack to cool completely.

BUTTERCAKE BAKERY BROWNIES

(V)

"A top seller at the bakery, these brownies are so much better than any made from a boxed mix. Espresso powder enhances the flavor of the chocolate without giving it a coffee taste." —LOGAN

2 sticks (8 ounces) butter, room temperature

1 cup (8 ounces) + 1½ cups (12 ounces) semisweet chocolate chips, divided

3 individually wrapped squares (3 ounces) of unsweetened chocolate (we recommend Baker's Chocolate squares, but any brand will do)

3 eggs, room temperature

1 tablespoon espresso powder (we recommend Medaglia d'Oro)

1 cup granulated sugar

1 tablespoon pure vanilla extract

½ cup all-purpose flour

½ teaspoon salt

1½ teaspoons baking powder

TRICK

For perfectly cut slices, pop the brownies in the freezer for 15 minutes and then slice with a sharp knife.

1. Preheat the oven to 325°F. Butter and flour a 9 x 13-inch pan.

2. Over medium heat, set up a double boiler by placing a metal or glass mixing bowl over a small pot of simmering water. Place the butter, 1 cup (8 ounces) of semisweet chocolate, and the unsweetened chocolate in the bowl over the simmering water, stirring a few times until it all melts and becomes smooth.

3. Remove chocolate mixture from heat. Set aside and cool to room temperature, about 30 minutes.

4. While the chocolate cools, in a medium bowl, whisk the eggs, espresso powder, sugar, and vanilla until combined.

5. Add the cooled chocolate to the egg mixture and stir to combine. Then add the flour, salt, and baking powder and stir to combine.

6. Fold in 1½ cups chocolate chips with a wooden spoon. Pour mixture into the prepared pan.

7. Bake for 30 minutes. Remove from oven and cool completely. Once cooled, cut into squares.

STORING AND FREEZING FOOD TRICKS

Get the scoop on the best ways to store and freeze leftovers and extra ingredients.

STORAGE TRICKS

MEAT AND POULTRY

BEEF: Keep beef in its original packaging and store in the fridge, on the bottom shelf where the fridge is at its coolest temperature. Ground beef can keep 1–2 days. Steaks and roasts should be cooked within 3–5 days of storage.

FISH: Fish is very perishable. It should only be stored for 1–2 days, tops. Store in the fridge, on the bottom shelf in a resealable plastic bag on top of a tray of ice. Best to keep the temperature at 32°F. (Most fridges are set to 40°F.) This will slow the enzyme breakdown.

PORK: Store in the fridge on the bottom shelf. Ribs, roast, steaks, and chops can be refrigerated for 3–5 days. All other pork parts should be cooked within 1–2 days.

POULTRY: Store in the fridge on the bottom shelf for 1–2 days.

DAIRY

BUTTER: Store butter in its carton on a shelf in the refrigerator rather than the door, because every time you open the door, the temperature fluctuates. Unopened, wrapped sticks of butter will keep for 1–3 months in the fridge and up to 6 months in the freezer. After it's been opened, go by the expiration date.

CHEESE: Store cheese in the fridge. If opened, wrap in wax paper and place inside a resealable plastic bag. It can keep for up to a week.

EGGS: Leave eggs in their carton on a shelf in the fridge and they will keep for up to five weeks.

MILK: Store it on the top shelf of the fridge in the back where the temperature is most constant.

PRODUCE

APPLES: The poison apple exists! Store apples on the counter, but keep them away from other produce. Apples give off ethylene gases that rot other produce if they are in close proximity.

ASPARAGUS: Stand upright in a resealable plastic bag, with either an inch of water at the bottom or with a wet paper towel wrapped around the base, and they will last 3-4 days.

AVOCADOS: Store on the counter. Once the avocados are slightly soft but not mushy, you can store them in the fridge for 2–3 days.

BANANAS: Store on the counter.

BERRIES: Keep berries in their original containers in the crisper drawer in the refrigerator. Don't wash them until ready for use. Strawberries and blueberries can last for a week. Blackberries and raspberries will only last a couple of days.

CARROTS: Store in the vegetable crisper drawer in the fridge for up to 3 weeks.

CITRUS: Avoid putting citrus fruits in the fridge. The low temperature takes away the aroma and flavor of the fruit. Store on the counter for up to 2 weeks.

CUCUMBER: Keep in the crisper drawer in the fridge for 4–5 days.

GARLIC: Store in a cool, dry, dark place and they will last up to 4 months.

HERBS, FRESH: Cut ½ inch from the stems. Stand stem ends in an old jam jar or mustard jar with a couple of inches of water in the bottom. Cover with a loose plastic bag and store in the fridge. Don't store basil in the fridge because it turns black. You can dry out your basil using our herb-drying trick. Fresh herbs will keep for 7–10 days in the refrigerator.

LEAFY GREENS: Store whole heads of leafy greens in the crisper drawer in the refrigerator unwashed. They will last for 5–7 days. Bagged greens will last 2–3 days after being opened.

ONIONS: Store in a container that will let air circulate throughout, like an aerated paper bag away from the sunlight. They will last up to 2 months. Do not store in plastic, as that will cause onions to sprout and get moldy. Sweet varieties have more water and will only last 2 weeks. Onions and potatoes taste great together—just don't store them together! Onions release a gas that will rot the potatoes. Cut onions should be wrapped tightly with plastic wrap and stored in the refrigerator for up to three days. Green onions should be kept in the crisper drawer of the refrigerator for up to a week.

PEPPERS: Store in the vegetable crisper in the refrigerator for 4–5 days.

POTATOES: Keep them out of direct sunlight and heat. Store in a cool, dry place for 2–3 months. Never put potatoes in the fridge—once they get cold, the starch turns to sugar. Do not wash potatoes before storing.

TOMATOES: Store on the counter out of direct sunlight. Do not refrigerate. Can keep for about three days.

TRICK

....

Dry out fresh herbs to make them last. Microwave on high for 30-second increments.

BAKING INGREDIENTS

ALL-PURPOSE FLOUR: Store in an airtight container in a cool, dry place for 6–12 months.

BAKING POWDER: Store in an airtight container in a dry place. Should last about 1 year, but check the expiration date on the container to make sure it's still fresh. If you're not sure if your baking powder is still good, add 1 teaspoon baking powder to $\frac{1}{3}$ cup hot water. If you see a bunch of foam form, it's still good. If not, time to buy a new container.

BAKING SODA: Store in an airtight container in a dry place for about 1 year, or up until the expiration date. If you have one open in your fridge to absorb odors, do NOT use it for baking. If you want to make sure it has rising power, mix $1\frac{1}{2}$ teaspoons with 1 tablespoon vinegar. If it fizzes, it's still got the power.

BROWN SUGAR: Store in an airtight container in a dry place for 4–6 months. If the brown sugar hardens, put a piece of white bread into the container and let it sit overnight and like magic,

the sugar will soften up. If you need to use the sugar right away, put the quantity that you need on a cookie sheet in the oven on 250°F for a few minutes to soften it up.

CORNSTARCH: Store in an airtight container in a cool, dry place for about 1 year, or up until the expiration date.

GRANULATED SUGAR: Store in an airtight container in a cool, dry place for 2 years.

POWDERED SUGAR: Store in an airtight container in a cool, dry place for 12–18 months.

VANILLA EXTRACT: Pure vanilla extract should be stored in an airtight container in a cool, dry place. Unopened, it can last up to 5 years. Opened, it should be used within 1 year.

YEAST, DRY PACKETS: Store in the fridge after opening. Should be used by the expiration date printed on the packaging. To test if the yeast is still active, stir 1 teaspoon sugar and 2 teaspoons yeast into a measuring cup filled with $\frac{1}{2}$ cup warm water. If the mixture doesn't foam and bubble in 10 minutes, then the yeast is no good anymore.

FREEZER TIMELINES

EVERYBODY FREEZE!
Wrapping and Labeling

ADD LABELS to items in your freezer and write the freeze date in permanent marker so you know how long it's been there.

USE HEAVY-DUTY FOIL, which is thicker than regular foil and less likely to snag and rip. Wrap it around food that is already sealed in plastic or parchment for an extra layer of protection.

FREEZER BAGS are resealable and made out of thicker plastic than regular storage bags. They also have a sturdier seal that won't crack open when exposed to freezing temperatures. Leave an inch free at the top of your storage bag when filling it with food so you can press out the air when sealing.

1 MONTH	Milk, ice cream, hot dogs, bacon
2–3 MONTHS	Casseroles, stews, bread, cooked pork or beef
6 MONTHS	Grated cheese, raw shrimp, cooked chicken
9 MONTHS	Muffins, cookies, fresh veggies, raw chicken parts
12 MONTHS	Raw whole chicken, steaks, butter, egg whites, bread crumbs

FREEZE GUIDE

THINGS YOU CAN FREEZE

Zero degrees Fahrenheit is the ideal freezer temp.

AVOCADOS – Enjoy guacamole any time of year! Save a ripe avocado by pureeing it in a food processor with 1 tablespoon lemon juice, packing in an airtight container, and freezing for later use.

BUTTER – Store whole sticks of butter in their paper wrappers in a freezer bag.

CASSEROLES – Before baking a casserole or lasagna, line the pan with aluminum foil, leaving a 4-inch overhang. Once the lasagna is baked and cooled, freeze it, then use the foil flaps to remove it from the pan. Tightly wrap it again with plastic wrap around the foil and pop it back in the freezer.

EGG WHITES – In an ice cube tray, freeze egg whites separately from the yolks. Yolks can't be frozen. Once frozen, store the cubes of egg whites in freezer bags.

ICE CREAM – After ice cream has been opened, press a piece of plastic wrap flat against the top of the ice cream to keep it creamy. If by some miracle you still have some left after a month in the freezer, toss it out, because ice cream is best eaten within a month after it's been opened.

LIQUOR – Spirits like vodka and gin will thicken a bit during the freezing process with the benefit of keeping the ice in cocktails from melting too quickly.

MILK – Pour into a freezer bag and freeze flat on cookie sheet. You can stand up the frozen bag to maximize space in the freezer later.

NUTS – Nuts spoil if stored at room temperature due to the high fat content. Place them in an airtight container or freezer bag and pop into the freezer for up to a year.

DO NOT FREEZE

CHEESE – Many fine, fresh cheeses will become gritty when frozen. Aged grated cheese, like Parmesan and cheddar, and blocks of processed cheese, like jack and provolone, can withstand the cold but after freezing are best used for melting.

COFFEE – The aromatic oils in the beans break down when frozen, resulting in a less flavorful cup.

ONIONS – They turn mushy and watery when thawed.

RAW POTATOES – They'll turn black and gritty. To freeze fresh potatoes, peel them, cut them in half, and put them in a pot of boiling water for 3–5 minutes. While they boil, fill a large bowl with water and ice. Use a slotted spoon to remove potatoes from the boiling water and place directly in the ice water bath for 10 minutes. Drain and pat the potatoes dry, place in a freezer bag, and remove all the air before sealing. They will keep up to a year.

WHOLE EGGS – Yolks become gummy when frozen.

THAWING TRICKS

IN THE FRIDGE: Set frozen food in its wrapper on a plate to catch drips. Foods thawed in the fridge will last 2–3 days more than those thawed using other methods. Defrosted poultry, fish, and ground meat can keep for 1–2 days in the refrigerator before cooking. Defrosted beef, pork, lamb, or veal can keep for 3–5 days in the fridge after thawing.

IN COLD WATER: Place food in an airtight bag and submerge in cold water. Change the water every 30 minutes. Don't use hot water, as it encourages bacteria growth. Food defrosted in water needs to be cooked immediately.

IN THE MICROWAVE: Unwrap foods and thaw using the defrost or low setting. If meats start to brown, remove and cool before continuing. Cook the food immediately after thawing.

ON THE COUNTERTOP: Bread and other frozen baked goods are safe to thaw on the counter. Keep them loosely covered with their wrapping from the freezer and place on a wire rack to prevent condensation and sogginess.

CHAPTER 2

WHY YOU SHOULD HEART YOUR CUISINART

RECIPES IN THIS CHAPTER

GUACAMOLE	56	HERB BUTTER	72
MELISSA'S BEAN DIP	58	BROWN SUGAR BUTTER	74
ROASTED SALSA	59	BERRY BUTTER	74
BRUSCHETTA	60	BLUE CHEESE SUNDRIED TOMATO BUTTER	74
ARUGULA PESTO	62		
SUNDRIED TOMATO PESTO	62	SRIRACHA-HONEY BUTTER	74
CREAMY COLESLAW	64	VEGGIE FRITTERS	75
QUINOA TABBOULEH	66	BLACK BEAN PATTIES	78
THREE-PEPPER JELLY AND BAKED BRIE	68	CHEESE DRAWER MAC AND CHEESE	81
		APPLE BLACKBERRY COBBLER	84
SCALLION PARMESAN DROP BISCUITS	70	RASPBERRY JALAPEÑO LIMEADE	86

THE CUISINART FOOD PROCESSOR

If there's one surefire way to whip up a quick meal, it's with the help of a Cuisinart food processor. Most busy people are overwhelmed by the chopping, grating, and slicing often required to make a dish from scratch. Good news—owning the Cuisinart food processor is like having a charming little robot for a prep cook. It might seem like cheating, but with prep work, if you're not looking for shortcuts, you're doing it wrong. In fact, most professional chefs use a food processor because it's the ultimate time saver. The quicker the ingredients are in order, the sooner you can eat.

A BIT OF HISTORY

The man behind the Cuisinart was Carl G. Sontheimer, an inventor and engineer who founded and sold two electronic companies prior to his grand cooking discovery. Born in New York but raised in France, Sontheimer loved French food and traveling to culinary expos. In 1971, the fifty-seven-year-old inventor attended a cooking show in France and came across a restaurant-style, heavy-duty appliance called the Robot-Coupe. This blender on steroids, designed by Pierre Verdun in 1963 for restaurant use, had a sharp blade inside a giant bowl and could grate, chop, slice, and puree ingredients with the push of a button. The proverbial lightbulb went off over Sontheimer's head. If home cooks had a machine like the Robot-Coupe, difficult dishes like French mousses could be prepared with much less effort. After obtaining distribution rights from Robot-Coupe, Sontheimer tweaked the design and scaled it down for countertops. The next step was to come up with a catchy name. Sontheimer always thought of French cuisine as an art—et voilà—the Cuisinart. The very first Cuisinart food processor made its debut in 1973 at the National Housewares Show in Chicago and was priced at a whopping $163. With a cost that steep, equivalent to about $800 today, sales were très slow. It wasn't until Craig Claiborne, famed food critic for *The New York Times*, wrote a glowing review that sales picked up. He called the machine the "most dexterous and versatile of food gadgets." Soon Julia Child and Jacques Pépin got on board, coming out in support of the genius invention and, in spite of the price tag, the Cuisinart started flying off the shelves. For the first time in history, cooks could set down their knives and let a wondrous little machine do the grunt work for them.

SO WHAT CAN IT DO?
AND WHY DO YOU NEED IT?

Available in multiple models with bowl capacities ranging from 3 cups for the mini chopper, and 7–20 cups for the food processor, the Cuisinart comes equipped with numerous attachments and blades. These features are built to tackle the most time consuming and mundane cooking tasks. We recommend a model that is at least 7 cups for home cooks, though we think the 9-cup model priced at $149 is, as Goldilocks would say, just right. With a shatterproof Lexan food bowl that is BPA-free (Yay! Fewer chemicals.), precision stainless steel blades, dishwasher-safe parts, an induction motor, and touch-pad controls, it's like a gift from the cooking gods. If you don't have one, put it on your wish list immediately.

GET TO KNOW YOUR CUISINART FOOD PROCESSOR

Parts and Features:

1. COVER AND FEED TUBE: The cover and feed tube needs to be snapped into place on the work bowl for the machine to function.

2. LEXAN SHATTERPROOF WORK BOWL: The detachable work bowl is where all the magic happens in your food processor. Resistant to hot and cold temperatures, it sits on the motor base and snaps into place.

3. SMALL WORK BOWL: Newer models of the Cuisinart food processor have a small bowl that nests inside the larger work bowl. The small bowl lifts out, leaving the large bowl ready to for bigger jobs. It's a nice addition to reduce cleaning in between steps.

4. SMALL CHOPPING BLADE: If using the small work bowl, there is a smaller chopping blade that fits inside.

5. REVERSIBLE STAINLESS STEEL SHREDDING DISC: Use stem adaptors with this disc. Works great for fine or medium shredding when grating cheese, cabbage, carrots, zucchini, and potatoes.

6. STAINLESS STEEL SLICING DISC: This blade is best for slicing stiffer fruits and vegetables like lemon, cucumbers, peppers, and potatoes. Use the attachable stem adaptor with this disc. *Safety note:* Pick up these blades by holding the outer rims like a CD, or use the finger holes on the Elite models.

7. DETACHABLE STEM ADAPTOR: If you're scratching your head wondering how the heck the slicing and shredding blades fit in the machine, the answer is the disc stem. The shredding and slicing discs attach to this stem, and it fits over the shaft in the center of the machine.

TRICK

You can turn on the machine, remove the large feed tube and the machine will stop. Add more food and reattach the large feed tube and it will start up again.

8. SPATULA: This flat-sided spatula makes it very easy to scrape down and around the sides of the bowl, which is important in order to mix in all the ingredients. You can also use any spatula you have on hand to scrape the bowl.

9. CLEANING TOOL: Use this double-sided cleaning tool to remove bits of food from the underside of the workbowl cover.

10. SMALL FOOD PUSHER AND 11. LARGE FOOD PUSHER: Use these parts (instead of your fingers) to push food against the blades and avoid trips to the emergency room. The small pusher works well for guiding slimmer fruits and vegetables, like carrots, cucumbers, or celery, toward the blade. The large pusher is ideal for wider ingredients, such as onions, apples, blocks of cheese, potatoes, etc. If you're making dressing, pour oil into the small pusher tube and it will drizzle through the tiny hole in the bottom and incorporate slowly to make a nice emulsification (essentially thickening your dressing).

12. STAINLESS STEEL "S" CHOPPING/MIXING BLADE: This is the blade you will most likely use all the time. It chops, minces, mixes, and purees. It works best for chopping herbs, onions, nuts, and bread crumbs, pureeing soups, grinding meat, processing garbanzo beans for hummus, and much more. *Safety note:* Pick up the chopping blade by the plastic hub/handle and match the outline on top of the hub with the shaft to fit it in place.

13. DOUGH BLADE: This little guy looks like the baby version of the "S" blade with the end sawed off. It's best for preparing yeast-based dough like pizza and bread. For less than 3 cups flour or for pie dough, use the "S" chopping blade.

In order to get even food slices use the slicing disk. Take a knife and cut the end off your ingredient so the flat surface can sit against the end of the slicing disc. Use the small or large pusher to put pressure on the ingredient and run it through the slicing disk. Start with food that is uniform in size; that will help keep slices consistent in size.

HOW TO USE A CUISINART FOOD PROCESSOR

Once you know what all the parts do and how they fit into the machine, the Cuisinart food processor is easy to use. If your machine is still in the box, step number one is to unwrap it and get it onto your counter. You'll notice instructions on the top flaps of the box. You can skim those, or if you're like us, just remove all the pieces and see if you can figure out what they do. When that doesn't work, read the rest of this chapter and we'll break it down for you.

Always pick up the blades by the plastic hub or rims, because they are crazy sharp. To assemble, start with the motor base. It houses a powerful induction motor that won't get bogged down even if it's kneading dough. Place the Lexan work bowl on the base, with the handle a little to the left of center, then turn it counterclockwise until it stops. You'll feel it click into place. To use the chopping blade, look at the top of the hub or handle and you'll see an outline in the shape of a half moon. Line that shape up with the shaft of the machine and it will sink into place, ready to chop. When using the slicers or shredders, attach the adapter stem, which fits over the shaft.

The machine gives you a PULSE button option, which means you can better control the size of the chopped ingredients by pushing on the PULSE button for quick intervals. Or if you're chopping garlic, onions, or veggies in the food processor, keep the motor running in the ON position and drop ingredients through the feed tube. Food will bounce around and won't get stuck in the blade or on the edge of bowl, and you'll get nice, even pieces.

HOW TO CLEAN YOUR CUISINART FOOD PROCESSOR

Wipe the base and buttons with a dishtowel and a non-toxic cleanser. If there are several steps to your recipe that require use of your Cuisinart, wash the bowl and all attachments with warm soapy water and rinse after each use. Dry with a dishtowel and replace all pieces for the next step.

Once your Cuisinart jobs are done for the day, rinse the bowl and blades in warm soapy water, removing any sticky food remnants, and then pop them in the dishwasher. If you don't have a dishwasher, fill the sink or a rubber dish tub with warm soapy water. Immerse all parts in the sink/tub and let soak for 10–15 minutes. Put on a pair of rubber gloves before reaching in to sponge off the blades to protect your hands from sharp edges. Run a soapy sponge over the blades and try to avoid using abrasive sponges. Most food should come off easily with a soft sponge. Rinse off the parts, dry with a dishtowel, and reassemble the machine so it's ready for its next job.

And now, chop, puree, shred, and knead your way through some of our favorite recipes!

GUACAMOLE

(GF, DF, V)

Who doesn't love guacamole? Perhaps it's a hit due to the magical properties of avocado, which lowers cholesterol and gives your skin a healthy glow. Or maybe it's just because it tastes so dang delicious. This foolproof recipe is not only easy to make, it's got a great kick to boot. Serve with crunchy tortilla chips, or scoop on top of tacos, burritos, or enchiladas.

juice from 2 limes

1 jalapeño, seeds and ribs intact, roughly chopped

2 cloves garlic

1 Roma tomato, roughly diced

½ red onion, roughly chopped

¼ cup cilantro

3 ripe avocados

salt and pepper to taste

TRICK

To tell if an avocado is ripe, give it a gentle squeeze; it should be slightly soft but not mushy. To ripen avocados more quickly, place them in a sealed paper bag with an apple or banana for 24 hours. The apple or banana will released ethylene gas, which speeds up the avocado ripening process.

1. In the food processor, combine lime juice, jalapeño, garlic, Roma tomato, red onion, and cilantro. Pulse 30 times until everything is in small chunks.

2. In a mixing bowl, mash the avocados with a fork to form a chunky mixture. Add the ingredients from the food processor to the avocados and stir to combine. Season with salt and pepper.

3. Serve immediately with tortilla chips or use as a topping on tacos, enchiladas, or burritos. If not serving immediately, take a piece of plastic wrap and push it against the top of the guacamole to keep it from turning brown. It can chill for an hour in the fridge before serving.

MELISSA'S BEAN DIP

(GF, V)

This recipe was contributed by guest chef Melissa Ehlke.

"Every family has that a recipe that you nostalgically associate with good times . . . pool parties in the backyard, summers by the lake, or simply catching up with friends over margaritas. This is ours. We've been making it for as long as I can possibly remember. The bowl is always licked clean and people beg for the recipe. It can be pulled together in a matter of minutes with ingredients typically found in the fridge and pantry, making it ideal for impromptu get-togethers." —MELISSA

1 can (16 ounces) refried beans

8 ounces sour cream

8 ounces cream cheese

1 packet taco seasoning

6 green onions, roughly chopped

1. Preheat oven to 350°F.

2. Grease an 8 x 8-inch baking pan with nonstick cooking spray

3. In the food processor, add all ingredients and let run until everything is incorporated, about 30 seconds.

4. Use a spatula to scrape mixture into the greased pan.

5. Bake for 30 minutes. Serve warm with tortilla chips.

TRICK

Save some calories and use low fat sour cream and cream cheese—no one will ever know!

ROASTED SALSA

(GF, DF, V)

"My friend Ruben owns a great Mexican restaurant called El Nopalito in Encinitas, and he refuses to disclose his delicious salsa recipe to me. Since it's hardly practical to drive from LA to San Diego every time I have a craving, I tried to decode it myself. This roasted salsa is about as close I can get." —LOGAN

3 cloves garlic, peeled

1 small yellow onion, quartered and slices separated

1–2 jalapeños (depending on your spice level), chopped into large chunks

1 pound cherry tomatoes (or another variety of small tomato)

1 teaspoon salt

½ teaspoon pepper

⅓ cup cilantro, chopped

4 green onions, chopped

TRICK

Avoid wilting the cilantro and green onions by adding after the salsa has cooled.

1. In a dry frying pan on medium heat, add the garlic, onion, and jalapeños. Shaking the pan a few times, roast the ingredients until small brown spots appear, about 5 minutes.

2. Put the garlic from the pan into the food processor. Add the tomatoes to the pan.

3. Continue cooking the tomatoes, onion, and jalapeños for an additional 5 minutes until the tomatoes start to show signs of roasting (browning in spots). Shake the pan a few times during this process so all the ingredients are evenly roasted.

4. Transfer all ingredients from the pan into the food processor and puree.

5. Place salsa in a mixing bowl, add salt and pepper, and place in your refrigerator to cool.

6. Once cool, add cilantro and green onions.

BRUSCHETTA

(GF, DF, V)

Bruschetta, pronounced "bru-sketta," originated in Italy as a clever way to salvage stale bread by adding a garlicky tomato mixture as a topping. Because this recipe packs such a zing, we love it on just about anything that needs a dose of flavor. And next time you pronounce it, belt it out like Luciano Pavarotti. Your guests will give you a standing ovation for the taste and your Italian accent. Serve with crostinis or chips, or on top of pasta or chicken to add a flavorful punch to simply prepared dishes.

2 cloves garlic

1 pound grape tomatoes (or other variety of small tomato)

12 medium basil leaves

1 tablespoon extra-virgin olive oil

1 tablespoon balsamic vinegar

½ teaspoon salt

¼ teaspoon pepper

1 teaspoon sugar

1. Turn ON food processor, and drop the garlic through the feed tube. Let it run/chop for 5 seconds.

2. Place the tomatoes, basil, olive oil, vinegar, salt, pepper, and sugar in the food processor and pulse 20 times until a chunky sauce forms. Serve cold. It can be made a day ahead and stored in the refrigerator until ready to serve.

TRICK

Make your own crostinis. Heat oven to 350°F and cut a baguette on the diagonal into half-inch thick slices. Place slices on a cookie sheet and drizzle with 2 tablespoons extra-virgin olive oil. Bake for approximately 5 minutes, until golden brown. Spoon bruschetta on top and serve.

PESTO TWO WAYS!

(GF, V)

Pesto sauce originated in Genoa in northern Italy and traditionally consists of pine nuts, garlic, basil, Parmesan cheese, and olive oil. The name comes from the Italian word *pesta* "to crush" or "to pound," because the sauce was made with a mortar and pestle. That was long before food processors came along and made everything one million times easier. These yummy alternatives to traditional basil pesto take just 5 minutes to whip up and taste great on pasta, crostini, chicken, or even as a sandwich spread.

ARUGULA PESTO

2 cups arugula

¼ cup walnuts, roughly chopped

½ cup grated Parmesan cheese

2 cloves garlic

¼ teaspoon salt

¼ teaspoon pepper

juice of ½ lemon

½ cup extra-virgin olive oil

salt and pepper to taste.

SUNDRIED TOMATO PESTO

½ cup sundried tomatoes in oil

1 clove garlic

¼ cup grated Parmesan cheese

¼ cup pine nuts

¼ teaspoon red pepper flakes

1 teaspoon dried oregano

1½ teaspoons red vinegar

¼ cup extra-virgin olive oil

salt and pepper to taste

1. In a food processor, pulse all ingredients except olive oil until a coarse puree forms.

2. Turn ON food processor and slowly add the extra-virgin olive oil through the small feed tube. Once all the oil has been incorporated, season with salt and pepper to taste.

Store in an airtight container in the fridge for up to a week. Or freeze portions in ice cube trays and once frozen, transfer to a resealable freezer bag and it will keep for up to three months.

TRICK

Store nuts in the freezer to keep them fresh for up to a year.

CREAMY COLESLAW

(GF, V)

The name "coleslaw" comes from the Dutch word for cabbage salad, *koolsalade*. There are many different varieties of this crunchy side dish, but our version wows a crowd with the brightness of its colors and flavors. A staple at every BBQ, it tastes great with tacos, sliders, or all by its cool lonesome.

SLAW MIX

½ head green cabbage, cored and cut into quarters

¼ head red cabbage, cored and cut into quarters

3-4 medium carrots, peeled

6 green onions, white and green parts (ends snipped), chopped

DRESSING

½ cup Greek yogurt

½ cup mayonnaise

3 tablespoons granulated sugar

2 tablespoons grated onion

2 tablespoons cider vinegar

2 tablespoons lemon juice

2 teaspoons Dijon mustard

½ teaspoon celery seeds

½ teaspoon salt

⅛ teaspoon pepper

3 dashes hot sauce

1. In a food processor with the slicing disc, lay cabbage horizontally in the large feed tube and use the large pusher to push down. Turn the machine ON. Repeat until all the red and green cabbage is sliced. Transfer sliced cabbage to a mixing bowl.

2. Remove the slicing disc and attach the shredding disc to the stem. Grate the carrots.

3. Add shredded carrots to the bowl and mix in the green onion.

4. Assemble all dressing ingredients in a container with a lid and shake to combine.

5. Add just enough dressing to the mixing bowl to coat the cabbage. Toss, and refrigerate for 1 hour before serving.

TRICK

Add bell peppers, sugar snap peas, chopped chicken, and our Sesame Dressing (page 25) to the slaw mix to turn this into a Chinese chicken salad.

QUINOA TABBOULEH

(GF, DF, V)

Tabbouleh is one of the most popular salads in the Middle East, western culture, and Haiti. If world peace were dependent on food, Tabbouleh might just be the great equalizer. Everyone loves it—and for good reason. It's zesty, tasty, and healthy. Traditionally made with bulgur wheat, ours is made with the super food, quinoa, which originated in South America and is high in protein and naturally gluten-free.

1 cup dry quinoa

1 clove garlic

¼ red onion, cut into chunks

1 bunch fresh parsley
(about 2 cups)

¼ cup fresh mint

1 cup grape tomatoes (or another variety of small tomato)

½ hothouse or English cucumber (or a regular cucumber with the seeds removed), cut in chunks

1 teaspoon salt

½ teaspoon pepper

¼ teaspoon ground allspice

⅓ cup extra-virgin olive oil

¼ cup lemon juice

TRICK

We recommend red quinoa, which has a slightly earthier flavor and a pretty color.

1. In a saucepot, cook quinoa according to package directions. Place cooked quinoa in a medium mixing bowl and set aside.

2. In a food processor, combine garlic, onion, parsley, and mint. Pulse 15–20 times until everything is finely chopped.

3. Add tomatoes and chunks of cucumber to the food processor. Pulse an additional 20 times until well combined.

4. Add the mixture into the bowl with the cooked quinoa. Add salt, pepper, allspice, olive oil, and lemon juice, and stir. Can be served cold or at room temperature.

THREE-PEPPER JELLY AND BAKED BRIE

(GF, V)

"This Three Pepper-Jelly is quickly becoming my favorite condiment. It's great on everything, including a grilled cheese sandwich, wings, biscuits, and even served over goat cheese or melted brie. This Baked Brie is a quick and tasty appetizer that'll impress your friends." —LOGAN

1 red bell pepper, seeds and ribs removed, cut into big chunks

2 jalapeños, seeds and ribs intact, cut into big chunks

1 cup apple cider vinegar

2 cups granulated sugar

1 tablespoon pectin powder

½ teaspoon red chili flakes

½ teaspoon salt

8-ounce wheel of brie (preferably triple cream)

1. In a food processor, turn ON machine and puree the bell pepper and jalapeños for 15 seconds, scrape down the sides with a spatula, and puree for another 15 seconds until the peppers are finely chopped.

2. Transfer pepper mixture to a saucepan, then add cider vinegar, sugar, pectin, chili flakes, and salt. Stir to combine.

3. On medium high heat, bring the mixture to a boil. Reduce heat to low and simmer (the bubbles will almost disappear except for a few small ones around the edge) until the liquid reduces to about 2 cups. This should take about 25 minutes.

4. Transfer to a covered container and chill. The jelly will thicken as it cools. It will keep for 3 weeks in the fridge. Stir the jelly before using.

5. Preheat oven to 350°F. Line a cookie sheet with parchment paper.

6. Place brie on cookie sheet. Bake for 10–12 minutes until it begins to ooze, not melt.

7. Use a spatula to transfer brie to a serving platter and spoon the Three-Pepper Jelly over the top. Serve warm with crackers.

SCALLION PARMESAN DROP BISCUITS

(v)

If there is a food from the heavens above, we suspect it's biscuits. Think about it—not only are biscuits delicious both naked or slathered with butter, they are also edible sponges, great for sopping up sauces or pushing spare bits of food onto your fork. Our savory Scallion Parmesan Drop Biscuits taste great with stews and chili but are also delicious solo.

2¼ cups all-purpose flour

2½ teaspoons baking powder

¾ teaspoon baking soda

½ teaspoon salt

2 teaspoons granulated sugar

6 tablespoons (3-ounces) cold unsalted butter, cut into small cubes

6 scallions, white and green parts, roughly chopped

1½ cups grated Parmesan cheese

1 cup buttermilk

TRICK

For a more traditional batch of biscuits, remove the scallions and Parmesan and add an extra ½ teaspoon salt.

1. Preheat oven to 450°F. Line a cookie sheet with parchment paper.

2. In a food processor, add flour, baking powder, baking soda, salt, sugar, butter, and scallions.

3. Pulse 20 times until coarse meal forms.

4. Turn the machine ON. Slowly stream the buttermilk through the small feed tube until just combined and a ball of dough forms. **Do not overmix, or the dough will become tough.**

5. Using a large ice cream scoop drop dough into 12 balls onto the cookie sheet (if using a small ice cream scoop, drop 24 dough balls) with some room in between each biscuit so they have room to spread.

6. Bake for 10–13 minutes, turning once (for small biscuits check after ten minutes).

Enjoy these the day you bake them.

COMPOUND BUTTERS

(GF, V)

It would be downright irresponsible to give you a biscuit recipe and not accompany it with some delicious flavored butters. Add a tasty boost to dishes or just eat these butters slathered on bread. Sweet or savory, there's something for everyone. If you're having friends over, chill the butter in ice cube trays or small ramekins to give them a nice shape.

HERB BUTTER

Serving Suggestion: Apply to chicken before roasting to boost flavor.

1 stick (4 ounces) of unsalted butter, room temperature

1 clove garlic, grated

zest from 1 lemon

1½ tablespoons mixed fresh herbs (parsley, basil, chives, thyme)

salt and pepper to taste

1. In a food processor, blend the butter until smooth.

2. Add the specific ingredients for each butter recipe and blend everything until well combined.

TRICK

To shape the butters into round discs, place butter in the center of a piece of plastic wrap. Fold the plastic over and roll into a log shape, twist the ends close. Refrigerate and slice into discs.

RECIPE CONTINUES ○——→

1. Herb Butter, 2. Brown Sugar Butter, 3. Blueberry Butter, 4. Blue Cheese Sundried Tomato Butter, 5. Sriracha-Honey Butter

BROWN SUGAR BUTTER

Serving Suggestion: Slather on pancakes or toast for a sweet breakfast treat.

1 stick (4 ounces) unsalted butter, room temperature

1 tablespoon packed brown sugar

¼ teaspoon pure vanilla extract

¼ teaspoon ground cinnamon

¼ teaspoon nutmeg, grated

pinch of salt

BERRY BUTTER

Serving Suggestion: Spread this on our Buttercake Bakery Orange Currant Scones (page 120–121) for a decadent treat.

1 stick (4 ounces) unsalted butter, room temperature

1 teaspoon granulated sugar

1 tablespoon of your favorite jam or jelly

BLUE CHEESE SUNDRIED TOMATO BUTTER

Serving Suggestion: Serve with grilled steak to give it a tasty zing.

1 stick (4 ounces) unsalted butter, room temperature

3 tablespoons sundried tomatoes in oil, roughly chopped

1 clove garlic, grated

2 tablespoons blue cheese, crumbled

6 medium basil leaves, roughly chopped

salt and pepper to taste

SRIRACHA-HONEY BUTTER

Serving Suggestion: Melt over grilled corn for a spicy/sweet kick.

1 stick (4 ounces) unsalted butter, room temperature

1 tablespoon honey

2 teaspoons sriracha (found in the international aisle of your market)

salt and pepper to taste

VEGGIE FRITTERS

(V)

Have you ever heard the expression "everything tastes better fried?" Well it's pretty much true. In this case, the combination of sweet potato, zucchini, and Parmesan already packs a flavor punch, but drop the mixture into a skillet with a bit of oil, and BLAM—fritterlicious! Serve with our Vinegar Dipping Sauce.

FRITTERS

1 large sweet potato, peeled and cut in half

2 large zucchini, cut in half

¼ yellow onion

⅓ cup all-purpose flour

¼ cup grated Parmesan cheese

1 egg

½ teaspoon baking powder

½ teaspoon salt

¼ teaspoon pepper

3 tablespoons vegetable or canola oil

VINEGAR DIPPING SAUCE

2 tablespoons lime juice (about 2 limes)

2 tablespoons rice vinegar (found in the international aisle of your market)

1 tablespoon extra-virgin olive oil

2 teaspoons granulated sugar

½ teaspoon sambal oelek (Asian chili garlic paste found in the international aisle of your market)

salt and pepper to taste

TRICK

Switch up the ingredients by swapping in shredded squash, corn kernels, or chopped spinach. You'll need 3 cups shredded veggies total, or 1½ pounds, before you wring out the liquid.

RECIPE CONTINUES ○——→

1. In a food processor with the shredding blade, place half of a sweet potato through the large feed tube, flat side against the blade, and use the large pusher to push down. Turn machine ON and push potatoes, zucchini, and onion through until all the veggies are shredded.

2. Over the sink, place a handful of the shredded veggies in a kitchen towel and twist into a ball to squeeze extra liquid out. Set aside wrung out portions in a mixing bowl. Continue to wring out handful size portions using the kitchen towel process until the entire mixture has been wrung out.

3. Place wrung out mixture in a mixing bowl and add flour, Parmesan cheese, egg, baking powder, salt, and pepper. Stir to combine.

4. Heat oil in the bottom of a heavy skillet over medium heat.

5. Use the small ice cream scoop to drop 4 balls of shredded veggies at a time into the hot oil. Flatten the patties with the back of the scoop to make them ½-inch thick.

6. Fry for 2–3 minutes until golden brown on the bottom and then flip the patties and fry for 2 minutes on the other side.

7. Transfer patties to paper towel-lined plates to drain any excess oil.

8. Repeat frying process until all the veggie mixture is used. You may need to add more oil as you go.

9. Serve warm with Vinegar Dipping Sauce. Combine all sauce ingredients in a small bowl and it's ready to serve.

BLACK BEAN PATTIES

(DF, V)

Preparing meals can be a head-scratcher when some of your diners are vegetarians and some are carnivores. Enter these hearty Black Bean Patties that are perfect for every palate. Black beans are a superfood with 15 grams of fiber and 15 grams of protein, which is equal to 2 ounces of chicken or a meatier fish like salmon. Combine that with walnuts, the world's other healthiest food (they are said to reduce cholesterol and risk of diabetes), and you're practically saving lives!

1 can (15 ounces) black beans, drained, rinsed, and patted dry (with ⅓ cup beans reserved for later)

¼ yellow onion, roughly chopped

1 clove garlic

¼ cup walnuts, roughly chopped

1 egg

pinch of red pepper flakes

½ teaspoon paprika

½ teaspoon hot sauce

½ teaspoon cumin

¼ teaspoon soy sauce

¼ cup panko (Japanese-style flaky breadcrumbs)

salt and pepper to taste

2 tablespoons extra-virgin olive oil

1. In the bowl of the food processor, combine the beans (minus the ⅓ cup), onion, garlic, and walnuts. Pulse 20 times.

2. Transfer mixture to a separate bowl and stir in the ⅓ reserved cup whole black beans, egg, red pepper flakes, paprika, hot sauce, cumin, soy sauce, panko breadcrumbs, salt and pepper. Mix ingredients together to combine well.

3. Form the mixture into 4 patties.

4. Heat the olive oil in a large sauté pan on medium heat.

5. Once the oil is hot, add the patties and cook about 4 minutes on each side until a crust forms. Cool on paper towels to absorb excess oil. Serve in a pita pocket with your favorite burger toppings.

TRICK

Place burger toppings like ketchup, mustard, pickles, tomatoes, and onions in a muffin tray. It keeps everything separated and organized—and looks cute to boot.

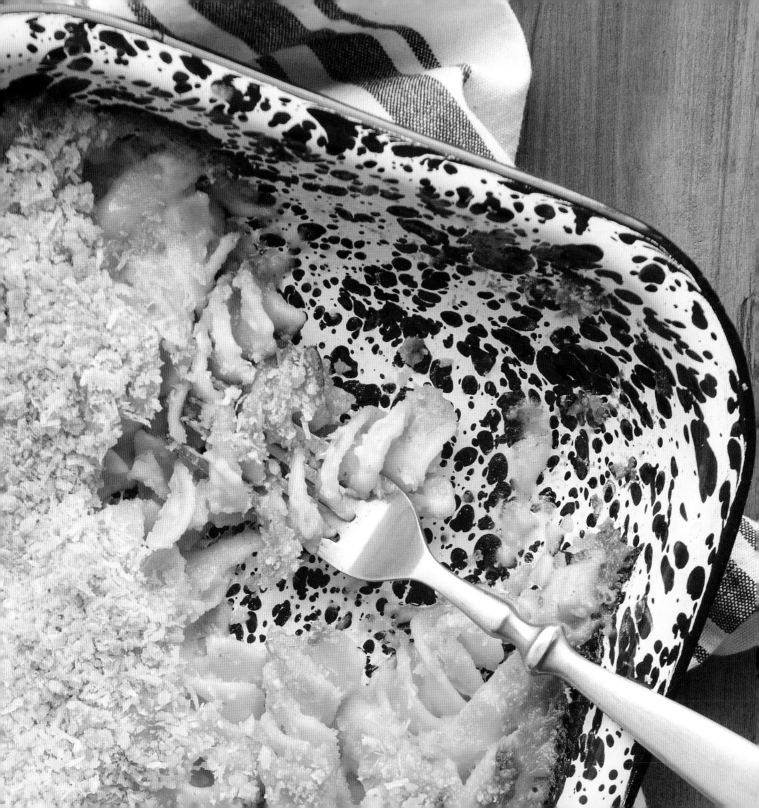

CHEESE DRAWER MAC AND CHEESE

(v)

"I cofounded the blog We Heart Mac and Cheese *and began a two-year odyssey in which I survived mainly on cheese and noodles. While I can't say it was great for my health, it did make me a veritable expert on the dish. The main drawback of my "research" was that I'd end up with a lot of scraps but not enough to replicate a recipe. One day, I decided to make a dish using all the leftover cheese in the drawer and Voilà: Cheese Drawer Mac and Cheese was born. This mac blows everyone away with its creamy nuttiness from the Gruyère, tang from the extra-sharp cheddar, and smoky Gouda accents. The butter cracker topping gives each bite a light crunch. Tell your guests to wear their stretchy waistband pants, because this mac and cheese is so insanely decadent, they'll want to eat at least two helpings."* —HILARY

MAC AND CHEESE

¾ cup (6 ounces) extra sharp cheddar

½ cup (4 ounces) gruyère

½ cup (4 ounces) smoked gouda

2 tablespoons (1 ounce) Parmesan cheese

2 cups 2% milk

¾ cup heavy cream

¼ cup all-purpose flour

3 tablespoons unsalted butter

1 teaspoon kosher salt

⅛ teaspoon pepper

¼ teaspoon cayenne

⅛ teaspoon ground nutmeg

10 ounces macaroni noodles or rigatoni or fusilli (any small pasta noodle will do)

CRUMB TOPPING

10 small butter crackers

4 ounces Parmesan cheese, grated

TRICK

Be sure to use smoked gouda and extra-sharp cheddar cheese to amp up the rich, tangy flavor of the dish.

RECIPE CONTINUES ⟶

1. Preheat oven to 350°F. Grease 8 x 8-inch baking dish with butter.

2. Use a food scale to weigh the different cheeses. In a food processor with the shredding blade, place the measured cheeses through the large feed tube and push down with the large pusher. Turn the machine ON, and the cheese will shred into the work bowl.

3. In a small saucepot, over low heat, warm the milk and cream but do not allow to it boil.

4. In a separate, larger pot, melt the butter over low heat, making sure not to burn it.

5. Add flour to butter and cook for 1 minute until the flour breaks down and creates a paste.

6. Slowly add in the milk and cream mixture to the butter and flour mixture, whisking like crazy for 8–10 minutes until it thickens and resembles a cream sauce.

7. Remove saucepan from heat and stir in all the cheese except the 4 ounces of grated Parmesan reserved for the topping, salt, pepper, cayenne, and nutmeg. Set aside.

8. Fill a stockpot with water and bring to a boil. Add the pasta. Cook for 3–5 minutes until pasta is al dente, a bit softened but still crunchy.

9. Use a colander to drain noodles and rinse in cold water. Add noodles to cheese sauce and stir well.

11. To make the topping, in a food processor with the chopping blade, grind crackers and 4 ounces of Parmesan cheese together into crumbs.

12. Transfer cheese and noodle mixture to baking dish and cover liberally with crumb topping mixture.

13. Bake for 30 minutes until the top is golden brown. Serve warm.

APPLE BLACKBERRY COBBLER

(V)

When early British settlers first landed on US soil, they couldn't find the ingredients needed to make traditional English pudding. Improvisation kicked in, and they covered stews with biscuits and dumplings. Those dishes eventually evolved into the tasty cobblers we know and love today. Light and scrumptious, this cobbler is a terrific summer dessert. Feel free to mix up the berries all year long. At Thanksgiving, go seasonal and substitute fresh cranberries for blackberries.

TOPPING

1½ cups all-purpose flour *

1½ sticks (6 ounces) cold unsalted butter, cut into small pieces

⅓ cup pecans, roughly chopped

½ cup granulated sugar

½ cup packed brown sugar

½ teaspoon salt

You can substitute gluten-free flour and it's still delicious.

FILLING

6 green apples (preferably Granny Smith), peeled, cored, and cut into wedges

1 cup blackberries

¼ cup granulated sugar

¼ cup packed brown sugar

juice from half an orange

1. Preheat oven to 350°F. Grease a 9 x 13-inch pan.

2. Place all topping ingredients in a food processor with the chopping blade. Pulse 20–30 times until coarse crumbs appear. Transfer to a mixing bowl and set aside.

3. In a separate mixing bowl, combine apple wedges, blackberries, sugar, brown sugar, and orange juice. Toss all the ingredients, coating the apples and blackberries well. Transfer mixture to the prepared baking pan.

4. Spread the topping over the fruit.

5. Place the baking dish on the foil-lined cookie sheet (this will help catch any drips from the cobbler). Transfer to the oven and bake for 50–60 minutes, until juices bubble around edge. Serve warm with vanilla ice cream.

TRICK

Cobbler can be made 1 day ahead and reheated at 350°F until the filling bubbles again, about 30 minutes.

RASPBERRY JALAPEÑO LIMEADE

(GF, DF, V)

Tart and spicy, this limeaid is refreshing over ice on a hot day. We use simple syrup to keep the grainy texture of granulated sugar out of the drink.

¾ cup + 4 cups water, divided

¾ cup granulated sugar

2 jalapeños cut in big chunks

1 cup fresh lime juice (about 15 limes)

1 cup fresh raspberries

1. To make the infused simple syrup, heat ¾ cup water, sugar, and jalapeños in a small saucepan over medium-low heat. Cook the mixture until the sugar dissolves, then turn off the heat. Let the liquid sit and infuse for at least 20 minutes.

2. Add the raspberries to the food processor. Turn ON for 30 seconds until puree forms. Set mixture aside.

3. In a pitcher, combine 4 cups water, lime juice, pureed raspberries, and ¾–1 cup of the jalapeño simple syrup (adjust amount depending on how sweet you like it.) Serve in glasses with ice.

TRICK

Mix in some tequila for a grown-up version.

CHAPTER 3

COOKIE SHEETS—NOT JUST FOR COOKIES ANYMORE

RECIPES IN THIS CHAPTER

GRANOLA 94

ROASTED CHICKPEAS 96

ROASTED TOMATO SOUP 98

CORNBREAD PANZANELLA 100

ROASTED CARROTS 102

LEMON DIJON ROASTED
BRUSSELS SPROUTS 104

BAKED SWEET POTATO FRIES 106

SPICY SHRIMP TACOS 108

INDOOR DRY RUB RIBS 110

OVEN-BAKED CHICKEN WINGS 112

If your cupboard isn't stocked with at least 2 cookie sheets, head over to your local grocery store or cooking supply shop and grab a couple, pronto. Priced between $5–$20, a standard cookie sheet (12 x 16 x 1-inch) made out of sheets of aluminum or stainless steel is as essential to your kitchen as your oven.

SO WHAT CAN IT DO? AND WHY DO YOU NEED IT?

As the name of this chapter suggests, a cookie sheet is a versatile tool with a ton of uses that most cooks have never even dared to dream about. These sturdy pans are perfect for roasting veggies, baking fish, crisping bacon, and so much more (see our handy usage guide on the following page). Some cookie sheets are made with a 1-inch rim around the edge. They also come in light and dark colors, made with thick or thin metals, or coated with a nonstick finish. A thick, light metal cookie sheet with a 1-inch rim is ideal because it is less likely to buckle under high heat, and light metal conducts heat the best. Have you ever pulled a batch of cookies from the oven and they look perfect on the top but the bottoms are charred? Dang, isn't that just the worst? Chances are you weren't using a light metal baking pan. For evenly browned cookie bottoms every time, use the light metal pan.

HOW TO USE YOUR COOKIE SHEETS

Make sure to cover the pan's entire surface with food as uniformly as possible and slowly heat the pan to prevent the metal from buckling. It helps to line light metal cookie sheets with parchment paper or a silicone baking mat* to keep food or baked goods from sticking. The best rule of thumb is to use a fully rimmed cookie sheet without a nonstick surface to keep everything on the pan when you take it out of the oven. Nonstick coatings tend to wear off after heavy use, and when you use parchment or foil you can avoid most sticky situations. If a recipe calls for a jelly roll pan, it requires essentially a slightly smaller (10 x 15-inch) rimmed cookie sheet. However, if you're not making an actual jelly roll, the two pans are interchangeable.

Silicone baking mats are enchanted sheets of woven fiberglass that prevent baked goods from sticking to cookie sheets. They are heat resistant up to 580°F Fahrenheit and run about $20. A great investment to streamline the cleanup time.

USES BEYOND BAKING COOKIES

ORGANIZING AND CARTING AROUND INGREDIENTS: Place all your ingredients on a rimmed cookie sheet before you get started. If you need to pick everything up and move to another counter or out to the BBQ, no problem.

CATCH DRIPS: Line cookie sheet with foil and place in the oven under bubbling lasagnas, cobblers, or casseroles to catch drips and keep the bottom of the oven clean. Or place a cutting board inside a cookie sheet before you slice cooked meats; if any juice drips off, it'll collect in the cookie sheet. No counter mess!

DRAIN FRIED FOODS: Once you remove fritters or anything fried or breaded from a pan, set the food on a cooling rack inside a cookie sheet to drain. This keeps the food from getting soggy.

ROAST MEATS: Set a cooling rack inside a rimmed cookie sheet and you've got yourself the perfect roasting or broiling pan for meats and poultry.

CRISP UP PIE OR QUICHE CRUSTS: Put a foil lined rimmed cookie sheet in the oven while it's preheating and allow it to warm up. Once the baking temperature is reached, place the pie carefully onto the warm sheet. Bake the pie on the sheet, and the pie bottom will get nice and crispy. The cookie sheet will also catch filling that oozes out of a bubbling pie.

COOK BACON MORE EVENLY: It's tough to cook bacon perfectly in a skillet because some pieces get crispy and others remain rubbery, especially if you're cooking a lot of bacon at one time. Line a rimmed cookie sheet with foil and cover the surface with bacon. You can make a larger quantity for a big group, and the strips will crisp up nice and even. Try adding a sweet/spicy glaze: spoon our Three-Pepper Jelly (page 68) over the bacon for the last five minutes of cooking time.

SHAKE POWDERED SUGAR: Place cakes or the Buttercake Bakery Lemon Bars (page 134–36) on a cooling rack on top of a cookie sheet and shake powdered sugar with reckless abandon. The cookie sheet catches all the sugar. Feel free to collect it and reuse for a second sprinkling.

EASY FREEZING: Use smaller cookie sheets or jelly roll pans to freeze portions on a flat surface and then transfer to freezer bags. Label bags with the freeze date.

- Pour soups, chili, and freezable liquids into freezer bags and lay on a cookie sheet to freeze flat. The flat bags will maximize space in the freezer.

- Let casseroles cool, wrap individual portions, and arrange on a cookie sheet in the freezer. Once they are frozen, transfer to a resealable plastic bag to maximize space.

- Freeze berries on a cookie sheet so they don't clump together and then place in a resealable plastic bag. They can keep up to three months.

- Make extra cookie dough ahead of time and freeze scooped balls of dough on a cookie sheet. Once the dough is frozen, store balls in an airtight freezer bag.

ROASTING TIPS

Roasting vegetables with olive oil and herbs in the oven draws out the natural flavors and creates a tasty caramelized exterior while still keeping the veggies moist. For every 2 pounds of vegetables, toss with 2–3 tablespoons extra-Zvirgin olive oil. Season and spread in a single layer on a rimmed cookie sheet. Roast at 400°F until tender and golden brown, flipping once during the cooking time. All ovens are different, so it's good to check for doneness at the early end of the suggested cooking time. Sprinkle with your favorite hardy herbs like sage, thyme, or Herbes de Provence. We've provided a veggie roasting guide below.

ROAST THESE VEGETABLES FOR 25-30 MINUTES

- Asparagus, trimmed
- Broccoli, cut into florets
- Brussels Sprouts, halved
- Carrots, peeled, whole if small, halved (if large)
- Cauliflower, cut into florets
- Cherry Tomatoes, whole
- Eggplants, sliced 1-inch thick or cut into wedges, sprinkled with salt and allowed to sit for 30 minutes, rinsed, and patted dry
- Mushrooms, whole or halved (if large)
- Onions, cut into wedges
- Sweet Potatoes, cut into wedges

ROAST THESE VEGGIES 35-45 MINUTES

- Acorn Squash, peel on or off, seeds removed, cut into wedges
- Butternut Squash, peeled, seeds removed, sliced ½-inch thick
- Fennel, trimmed and cut into wedges
- New Potatoes, halved (if large) or whole (small)
- Parsnips peeled, halved if large or whole
- Russet Potatoes, cut into wedges
- Shallots, peeled

HOW TO CLEAN YOUR COOKIE SHEETS

Most cookie sheets are too big to fit in the dishwasher but are relatively easy to clean with soapy water and a non-abrasive sponge. If you have some sticky bits that won't come off with the sponge, fill the pans with water and soap and let soak for 20–30 minutes. Then clean with a sponge, rinse, and dry.

Now put those cookie sheets to use!

GRANOLA

(GF, DF, V)

Granola was originally called Granula, which is reminiscent of Dracula and should probably be pronounced with a thick Transylvanian accent just for fun: Grrra-NUU-lahh bwhahahahahah. Invented in 1894, the first recipe was made with graham flour. It wasn't until 1951 that a German guy named Willie Pelzer moved to Canada, brought oats into the equation and created the "Crunch Granola," we know and love today. This homemade version is sweet and spicy from the ginger and cinnamon and tastes great with milk or yogurt.

3 cups old fashioned rolled oats (not quick oats)

1 cup assorted chopped nuts (pick 1 or mix: pecans, walnuts, almonds, cashews)

3 tablespoons packed brown sugar

¾ teaspoon ground cinnamon

½ teaspoon ground ginger

¼ teaspoon salt

⅓ cup honey

2 tablespoons vegetable oil

1 cup assorted dried fruit* (pick 1 or mix: raisins, dates, apricots, cherries, cranberries)

Feel free to customize by adding coconut, additional spices, citrus zest, and seeds.

1. Preheat oven to 300°F. Line a rimmed cookie sheet with foil.

2. In a mixing bowl, stir together all ingredients *except* the dried fruit.

3. Spread mixture evenly on the prepared cookie sheet and bake until golden, about 40 minutes. Stir the mixture 2 or 3 times while baking to make sure it cooks evenly.

4. Remove the mixture from oven and allow to cool slightly. Then combine with the dried fruit. Serve at room temperature.

TRICK

If not eating right away, slide a large resealable plastic baggie over the foil, and shake the granola loose for a quick and easy cleanup. Can be made ahead of time and stored for 1 week.

ROASTED CHICKPEAS

(GF, DF, V)

At 7,500 years old, the chickpea deserves mad respect for being the original gangster of cultivated legumes. And like all good tough guys, this one has a bunch of aliases like "garbanzo bean," "ceci bean," and "Bengal gram." Whatever you call them, they're high in protein and iron but low in fat. Roasted and spiced, this snack has a great kick from the cumin and is addictive and healthy.

2 cans (30 ounces total) chickpeas

2 tablespoons extra-virgin olive oil

½ teaspoon lemon juice

1 teaspoon ground cumin

½ teaspoon paprika

¾ teaspoon salt

¼ teaspoon pepper

1. Preheat oven to 400°F. Line a cookie sheet with a silicone baking mat or parchment paper.

2. Drain chickpeas in a small colander. Rinse the chickpeas with water and pat dry with paper towels.

3. In a small mixing bowl, combine olive oil, lemon juice, cumin, paprika, salt, and pepper. Add the chickpeas and stir to coat.

4. Spread the chickpeas in a single layer on the cookie sheet and roast for 35–45 minutes, shaking the sheet a few times during cooking, until lightly golden. Serve warm or at room temperature. These are best if eaten the same day.

TRICK

The perfect snack alternative for people with nut or wheat allergies. Sprinkle on top of a salad instead of croutons.

ROASTED TOMATO SOUP

(GF, DF, V)

The very first recipe for tomato soup appeared in Maria Parloa's *The Appledore Cook Book* in 1872. Parloa, a native of Massachusetts, worked as a cook in private residences and hotels as a young woman and later founded two cooking schools. She even got to be a spokeswoman for the Baker Chocolate Company (coolest job ever) and is considered to be the first "celebrity chef." Maria's recipe required 3(!!) hours of boiling! But thanks to our slow-roasting tomato trick, which caramelizes the sugars and enhances the flavors, this soup can be made in a fraction of the time, and it still tastes as sweet and creamy as if you stood over a hot stove all day.

2½ pounds plum tomatoes (about 14), cut in half

2 yellow onions, sliced into ½-inch half-rounds

6 cloves garlic, coarsely chopped

2 tablespoons sugar

2 teaspoons salt

2 teaspoons pepper

⅓ cup extra-virgin olive oil

1 quart chicken stock or veggie stock

3 tablespoons tomato paste

¼ cup fresh basil leaves, rough chopped

⅛ teaspoon cayenne

TRICK

For the leftover tomato paste, measure 1-tablespoon portions and drop them into ice cube tray slots to freeze. Once frozen, transfer to resealable plastic bags for future use. You do not need to thaw them first.

1. Pre-heat oven to 450°F.

2. Place halved tomatoes, cut side up, on the 2 cookie sheets. Then add the onions and garlic to the tomatoes. Sprinkle the tomatoes evenly with the sugar, salt, pepper, and extra-virgin olive oil.

3. Place cookie sheets in the oven and roast for 25–30 minutes, or until the tomatoes begin to get brown spots.

4. Transfer all contents from cookie sheets to a stockpot. Add the chicken or veggie stock, tomato paste, basil, and cayenne.

5. Bring to a boil over medium high heat, then reduce heat to a simmer and cook for an additional 20 minutes.

6. Use a food processor, blender, or immersion blender to puree the soup. If you are using a food processor or blender, transfer soup to the machine but only fill the bowl halfway to prevent the soup from leaking. Turn the machine ON and run until smooth. Transfer pureed soup to a separate bowl and finish pureeing the rest of the cooked soup. Once it's all pureed, transfer it back to the pot and reheat over low.

7. Season with salt and pepper and serve.

CORNBREAD PANZANELLA

(v)

Tuscan bread salad, also known as panzanella, has been around since the sixteenth century. At least that's when the artist–poet Bronzino wrote a ditty about his love of toasted bread, tomatoes, and onions. Typically made with stale Italian bread, our version uses cornbread, which adds a sweet contrast to the tang of the tomatoes and gives it a bit of a southern flair.

1½ pounds (about 6 cups) prebaked or store-bought cornbread, cut into cubes

3 tablespoons extra-virgin olive oil

1 cup cherry tomatoes (about ⅓ pound), halved

1 cucumber, chopped into small cubes

1 bell pepper, cut into a medium dice

½ red onion, sliced into ¼-inch half-rounds

¾ cup blue cheese crumbles

Basil Balsamic Dressing (page 25)

1. Preheat oven to 400°F. Place cornbread cubes on a cookie sheet and toss with extra-virgin olive oil.

2. Bake for 10–15 minutes, tossing once during baking, until the edges are crisp.

3. In a large bowl, combine baked cornbread, tomatoes, cucumber, bell pepper, red onion, and blue cheese crumbles with the Basil Balsamic Dressing. Toss to coat and serve.

TRICK

Choose any type of bread and follow steps 1 and 2 to make your own croutons. Combine croutons and Romaine lettuce leaves with our Eggless Caesar Dressing (page 26) to make a Caesar salad.

ROASTED CARROTS

(GF, DF, V)

Carrots are rich in beta-carotenes and Vitamin A, and they help keep your eyesight healthy. But eating a raw carrot only releases 3 percent of beta-carotenes during digestion, so the best way to get the maximum nutrients is to cook carrots. This delicious roasted version with citrus, pine nuts, and green onions has just the right balance of spicy and sweet with the added bonus of nutrients galore.

1½ pounds heirloom or regular carrots, peeled and halved lengthwise

3 tablespoons + 1 tablespoon extra-virgin olive oil, divided

¼ cup pine nuts

2 cloves garlic, grated

¾ teaspoon ground cumin

¾ teaspoon ground coriander

⅛ teaspoon red pepper chili flakes

1 orange

4 scallions (just the white ends), thinly sliced

TRICK

Check your farmer's market for heirloom multi-colored carrots to incorporate a rainbow palette into the dish.

1. Preheat oven to 400°F.

2. In a large mixing bowl, combine carrots, 3 tablespoons extra-virgin olive oil, pine nuts, garlic, cumin, coriander, and chili flakes.

3. Transfer carrot mixture to a cookie sheet and spread out in a single layer.

4. Roast until tender, about 25–30 minutes. Check them about 15 minutes in, and flip carrots so both sides get browned.

5. While the carrots roast, use a paring knife to cut away the outside layer of the orange (peel and white pith.) Cut on both sides of each segment, freeing the segment from the membrane. Place the segments in a bowl, and squeeze the juice out of the orange membrane into the bowl.

6. Stir in scallions and remaining 1 tablespoon extra-virgin olive oil.

7. To serve, arrange carrots on a platter and spoon the orange mixture over the top.

LEMON DIJON ROASTED BRUSSELS SPROUTS

(GF, V)

Brussels sprouts are one of those vegetables that are, for the most part, universally loathed by children and loved by adults. There are the rare exceptions, like First Lady Michelle Obama, who hates these little cruciferous veggies. We assume she's never tried Lemon Dijon Roasted Brussels Sprouts, because if she had, she might change her tune. Tangy with just a hint of sweetness and a nice crisp, they hit the spot.

1½ pounds brussels sprouts, ends trimmed and cut in half

2 tablespoons extra-virgin olive oil

zest and juice from 1 lemon

1 teaspoon Dijon mustard

1 teaspoon packed brown sugar

¾ teaspoon salt

½ teaspoon pepper

½ teaspoon dried thyme or 6 fresh thyme sprigs

½ cup grated Parmesan cheese

Brussels sprouts range in size. If they're on the small side you'll need to decrease the cooking time by approximately 5 minutes and if they are large, you will have to increase the time by 5 minutes.

1. Preheat oven to 400°F. Line cookie sheet with foil and spray with nonstick cooking spray.

2. In a mixing bowl, combine brussels sprouts, olive oil, lemon zest and juice, Dijon mustard, brown sugar, salt, pepper, and thyme. Toss to combine.

3. Place the brussels sprouts cut side down on the prepared cookie sheet.

4. Roast for 15 minutes, then using a pair of tongs or spatula, flip the brussels sprouts and cook for an additional 10 minutes. Remove pan from the oven and sprinkle Parmesan cheese on top, then roast for an additional 5 minutes.

5. Serve warm or at room temperature.

BAKED SWEET POTATO FRIES

(GF, DF, V)

Have you ever tried to eat just one sweet potato fry? It's impossible. With just the right mix of salty, crunchy, and sweet, sweet potato fries are on our list of favorite foods. This baked variety manages to preserve the fried crisp texture but with just a fraction of the calories. Dip them in our Chimichurri Sauce (page 20) for an added flavor kick.

4 small sweet potatoes (about 2 pounds), skins on, ends trimmed, and cut into ½-inch thick sticks (try to make the sticks the same size so they cook evenly)

2 tablespoons cornstarch

1 teaspoon salt

½ teaspoon pepper

½ teaspoon chili powder

3 tablespoons extra-virgin olive oil

TRICK

Using cornstarch helps absorb moisture and achieve that delicious crunch. Substitute russet potatoes for sweet potatoes to make spicy french fries. Slice the potatoes into thin strips to get them extra crispy.

1. Preheat oven to 450°F. Line 2 rimmed cookie sheets with foil and spray lightly with nonstick cooking spray.

2. In a resealable plastic bag, combine sweet potatoes, cornstarch, salt, pepper, and chili powder. Seal bag and shake potatoes to coat evenly. Add olive oil to the bag and shake again to coat the fries.

3. Divide fries among the prepared cookies sheets. Do not crowd pan. The fries will steam and won't get crispy if they are too close together. Place cookie sheets on the middle rack and top rack.

4. Bake for 15 minutes and use tongs to flip fries over. Move the top pan to the middle rack and the middle pan to the top rack to ensure even crispiness. Bake 10-15 more minutes, until golden brown. Serve warm.

SPICY SHRIMP TACOS

(GF, DF)

These spicy shrimp baked in the oven pack a flavor punch from the sriracha hot sauce and citrus juices. Sriracha, named after the city of Si Racha in the Chonburi Province of Eastern Thailand, is made from chili pepper paste, distilled vinegar, garlic, sugar, and salt. It's a great condiment staple to keep at the ready when you need a dash of heat and zing in your dishes. Serve these shrimp with warm tortillas, cilantro, shredded lettuce or cabbage, limes, salsa, and radishes.

½ cup orange juice

¼ cup lime juice

½ cup cilantro

1 tablespoon sriracha (found in the international aisle of your market)

¼ cup extra-virgin olive oil

2 cloves garlic

3 green onions (white and green parts), ends trimmed

½ teaspoon salt

1 teaspoon chili powder

2 pounds large uncooked shrimp

1. Place all ingredients except the shrimp in food processor with the chopping blade.

2. Blend until smooth, about 30 seconds

3. Pour mixture into a resealable plastic bag and add shrimp.

4. Seal bag and marinate in the refrigerator for 1–2 hours (but not longer).

5. Preheat oven to 400°F. Remove shrimp from marinade and place on a cooling rack inside the cookie sheet. Bake for 3–5 minutes until firm, pink, and cooked through.

TRICK

Setting a cooling rack inside a rimmed cookie sheet creates a shallow broiling pans to help achieve a more even cook by letting the air circulate.

INDOOR DRY RUB RIBS

(GF, DF)

This recipe was contributed by guest chef Alison Levant.

"One sweltering summer day in LA when it was too hot to stand outside and man the grill, I came up with this alternative to barbecuing. These ribs baked in the oven are so easy and delicious, I vowed never to sweat over a grill again! The secret to making the meat fall off the bone is to cook them low and slow. They are perfect as is, but feel free to serve them with your favorite BBQ sauce." —ALISON

2 racks of baby back ribs (silver membrane on back side of bones removed)

1 batch Dry Spice Rub (page 16)

1. Preheat oven to 300°F. Line a rimmed cookie sheet with foil.

2. Season the ribs by sprinkling the dry rub all over the ribs and massaging the rub into the pork so it evenly coats the meat (front, back, and sides).

3. Place the ribs meat side up on the foil-lined sheet and bake 1½–2 hours, or until a knife inserted in the meat slides easily between the bones.

4. Remove from oven, and let the meat sit for 10 minutes. Use a chef's knife to slice between the bones into individual ribs. Serve warm.

TRICK

To enhance the flavor, step 2 can be done a day ahead. Wrap the seasoned ribs in foil and refrigerate. Allow the ribs to reach room temperature before you bake them.

OVEN-BAKED CHICKEN WINGS

The high season for chicken wings is January through March when sports fans ingest billions of these little fried guys like they're going extinct. If you love crispy wings but hate the mess of frying, this recipe is deep-fry-free! With the signature crunchy texture on the outside, these wings stay nice and juicy on the inside and have a lot less calories. Go Team!

CHICKEN WINGS

4 pounds chicken wings and drumettes, tips removed, flats and drumettes separated

1 tablespoon salt

1 tablespoon baking powder

SRIRACHA LIME SAUCE

½ cup sriracha (found in the international aisle of your market)

2 tablespoons honey

zest and juice from 1 lime

HOT HONEY CILANTRO SAUCE

½ cup honey

zest and juice from 2 limes

2 cloves garlic, grated

2 tablespoons soy sauce

2 teaspoons red pepper flakes

2 tablespoons cilantro, chopped

1 teaspoon salt

1 teaspoon pepper

1. Line 2 rimmed cookie sheets with foil and spray with nonstick cooking spray.

2. Place all the ingredients in a resealable plastic bag, seal it, and shake to coat the wings.

3. Spread the wings out on the prepared cookie sheets and let sit in the open air for 1 hour.

4. Preheat oven to 450°F.

5. Place the cookie sheets in the oven and bake for 20 minutes. Flip the wings using tongs, and cook for 20 minutes more.

6. To make sauces, mix all ingredients in a small bowl and toss with wings. Serve immediately.

TRICK

The baking powder and salt draw out the moisture from the chicken skin to give the wings a nice crisp.

CHAPTER 4

TIME FLIES WITH A MICROPLANE

RECIPES IN THIS CHAPTER

BUTTERCAKE BAKERY ORANGE CURRANT SCONES	120	TANDOORI SALMON SALAD	130
		BACKYARD CITRUS CHICKEN	132
FETA DIP	122	BUTTERCAKE BAKERY LEMON BARS	134
GRILLED ASPARAGUS WITH TRUFFLE OIL	124	CLASSIC CHOCOLATE PUDDING	137
CREAMED SPINACH	126	PANNA COTTA	140
COLD ASIAN PEANUT NOODLE SALAD	128	VELVET HAMMER SANGRIA	142

THE MICROPLANE

If you heard the word Microplane and envisioned a tiny puddle-jumping aircraft that shuttles terrified passengers to remote destinations, do not despair. The Microplane featured in this chapter has nothing to do with air travel but certainly makes times fly. This handy zester/grater will soon become your best friend in the kitchen. Made of surgical-grade stainless steel and affixed to a comfortable handle, the Microplane grinds spices, grates cheese, minces garlic and ginger, zests citrus, shaves chocolate, and so much more. Say goodbye to the fear of shredding your newly manicured nails on a standard box grater.

A BIT OF HISTORY

In 1990, Richard and Jeff Grace, brothers and founders of a photochemical machining company, spent a lot of time avoiding bumping into the super sharp scrap metal lying around their shop. But then it occurred to them that the metal might actually be used to cut something on purpose. After etching small holes into a piece of metal, they ran it across different surfaces to see how well it could cut and shave. It turned out to be the ultimate tool for shaping and cutting wood, and PRESTO, the Microplane wood rasp came to be. So what does this have to do with cooking? Well, in 1994, a woman named Lorraine Lee attempted to make an Armenian orange cake. She became fed up with the imprecision of her box grater, grabbed her husband's brand new Microplane wood rasp, slid it across the orange peel and was stunned by how deftly it zested the orange into thin shreds. Her husband was selling the rasps at his hardware store, and after Lorraine's discovery, they updated the tool description to include zesting. Now tons of chefs and home cooks are extremely grateful.

SO WHAT CAN IT DO? AND WHY DO YOU NEED IT?

Available in a range of sizes and colors, this affordable zester/grater, ranging in price from $8–$20, is a favorite amongst pros and home cooks, because it does such a beautiful job of shredding ingredients into super fine threads. Long and sleek, it fits right into a drawer or in a countertop gadget container.

HOW TO USE A MICROPLANE

1. Set up a cutting board, large bowl, or plate under your Microplane to catch all the fine shavings.

2. Hold the grater by the handle at an angle. Make sure the smooth side is facing up and the sharp grating blades face the back.

3. Press the food against the smooth side and move the food down the blade. Hold the Microplane steady.

4. You should only grate down; otherwise you push in the teeth and dull them against the blade.

ITEMS WE LOVE TO MICROPLANE

CHEESE: For hard cheese, use a medium Microplane. For soft cheese, use a wider version. Grate cheese right after you remove it from the fridge. Once it warms up, it softens and is much harder to grate evenly.

CITRUS: Microplane makes a version just for citrus that has two peeling blades on the opposite end of the handle. Make sure to use only the yellow or orange skin/rind of lemons and oranges for zesting, and avoid the white pith, which tastes bitter.

GARLIC: Use the finer texture tool to grate cloves of garlic, but to avoid "garlicifying" all your future ingredients, be sure to clean your Microplane well.

GINGER: Use the fine to medium Microplane for ginger. Freeze ginger ahead of time for easier grating.

JALAPEÑO PEPPERS: Use a medium textured grater. Be sure to clean well after use to avoid transferring heat to other ingredients.

WHOLE NUTMEG: Use a super fine Microplane to grate this spice into your fall desserts and dark bitter greens.

HOW TO CLEAN YOUR MICROPLANE

Use a dish brush and dish soap to remove bits of food. If you have a dishwasher, run it through a cycle to get rid of food smells and tastes, especially when grating garlic or jalapeño peppers. If you don't have a dishwasher, let it soak in soapy water for 15–20 minutes and scrub with a dish brush.

And now, Microplane your way through some of our favorite recipes . . .

BUTTERCAKE BAKERY ORANGE CURRANT SCONES

(V)

Is it any wonder that the comforting and delicious scone is celebrated as the star of tea services all over Great Britain? This Buttercake Bakery variety, with orange zest and currants, will make you feel as if you've been transported to Scotland, the actual birthplace of this bready treat. Serve these warm on their own, or as they do in the UK, with jam and clotted cream. And if these scones inspire you to take a trip to Scotland, you'll need to order a skon (rhymes with gone) when you get there because that's how the Scots pronounce it.

3 cups all-purpose flour, plus more for dusting surface

⅓ cup granulated sugar

2½ teaspoons baking powder

½ teaspoon baking soda

¾ teaspoon salt

¾ cup (6 ounces) unsalted butter, cold, cut into cubes

zest from 1 orange*

¾ cup currants*

1 cup buttermilk

....

*You can also substitute lemon/candied ginger, orange/cranberry, or lemon/blueberry to mix up the flavor.

1. Preheat oven to 400°F. Line the cookie sheet with parchment paper.

2. In a food processor, combine flour, sugar, baking powder, baking soda, salt, and butter and pulse until mixture has a sand-like texture.

3. Transfer mixture to a large bowl, creating a well in the center with your fingers. Add orange zest, currants, and buttermilk to the center. Stir until all the flour mixture is incorporated and can be formed into a ball.

4. Place dough ball onto a floured work surface, and with a rolling pin, roll out dough into a 1½-inch thick disk.

5. Use a chef's knife to cut the dough into 12 triangular pie-shape pieces.

6. With a pastry brush, brush the scone tops with buttermilk and sprinkle with sugar. Bake on the parchment-lined cookie sheet for 20 minutes, until tops are golden brown. Serve warm or room temperature.

TRICK

You can make a double batch and freeze half. Place the scones in a single layer in a resealable plastic bag. No need to defrost the dough before baking—just pop scones in the oven and bake for an extra two minutes.

FETA DIP

(GF, V)

Enjoy the flavors of the Mediterranean in this yummy dip made with tangy, salted Greek feta cheese and briny kalamata olives, named after the city where they are grown in southern Greece. Pair it with pre-made hummus and serve with crackers or sliced veggies as an appetizer before dinner or any casual get-together!

¾ cup pitted kalamata olives

½ cup parsley

½ red onion, roughly chopped

1 clove garlic

½ teaspoon fresh thyme

½ teaspoon fresh rosemary

3 tablespoons extra-virgin olive oil

zest and juice from 1 lemon

10-ounces good quality Greek feta cheese

1. In a food processor, combine olives, parsley, red onion, garlic, thyme, rosemary, olive oil, zest, and lemon juice and pulse 20 times.

2. Add feta and pulse 20 more times.

3. Transfer to a serving bowl. Serve chilled with crackers or veggies.

TRICK

To store feta, put the cheese in the corner of a small resealable plastic bag and pour just enough oil up the sides. Place the bag in a cup and press down on the cheese to force excess oil over the top. Will keep up to 4 weeks.

GRILLED ASPARAGUS WITH TRUFFLE OIL

(GF, V)

Asparagus is a superfood, rich in antioxidants, fiber, folate, and vitamins A, C, E, and K, and it is said to slow the aging process. This elegant side dish looks great on a plate and has the added benefit of keeping you and your guests looking young, healthy, and glamorous.

1 pound asparagus (medium stalks), tough ends trimmed

1 tablespoon extra-virgin olive oil

salt and pepper to taste

zest from 1 lemon

3 tablespoons grated Parmesan cheese

1 tablespoon black truffle oil

1. Turn on grill or grill pan to high heat.

2. Toss asparagus with olive oil, salt, and pepper. Place asparagus on the grill or grill pan and cook 3-5 minutes, until tender and char marks appear.

3. Transfer asparagus to a serving platter and top with lemon zest, grated Parmesan, and black truffle oil. Can be served warm or at room temperature.

TRICK

Truffle oil is olive oil infused with the flavor of truffle mushrooms and gives food a rich, earthy flavor. It's delicious tossed with french fries and Parmesan cheese too. It can be found in gourmet markets.

CREAMED SPINACH

Name any vitamin and there's a good chance it's found in spinach. Packed full of nutrients like calcium, folate, and protein, it makes sense that Popeye achieved superhuman strength after chugging down a can of these leafy greens. Put our creamy spinach on the menu, and an impromptu arm wrestling contest might break out before dessert. "My first word was Popeye, which means I was destined to love spinach. It's the perfect side dish for any meal, but I always serve it at Thanksgiving." —LOGAN

1 (16-ounce) package frozen chopped spinach, thawed

2 slices bacon, chopped

½ medium yellow onion, chopped

1 clove garlic, grated

2 tablespoons flour

¼ teaspoon seasoned salt (e.g., Lawry's)

¼ teaspoon pepper

¼ teaspoon freshly grated nutmeg

1 cup whole milk

TRICK

Freeze bacon before you slice it to make it easier to cut. If you want to keep the recipe vegetarian, omit the bacon and cook the onions in 1 tablespoon extra-virgin olive oil.

1. Defrost spinach according to package. Drain in a colander over a sink and press a wooden spoon against the leaves in the strainer to squeeze out as much water as possible.

2. In a sauté pan over medium heat, cook bacon and onion until tender, about 6 minutes. Then add garlic and cook for 2 more minutes.

3. Add flour, salt, pepper and nutmeg to bacon mixture in the pan and stir.

4. Once well mixed, slowly add the milk into the pan and cook until thickened. Then add the spinach. Cook, stirring the mixture for about 2 minutes, until well combined and heated through. Transfer to a serving dish and serve warm.

COLD ASIAN PEANUT NOODLE SALAD

(DF, V)

On a warm summer night, the spicy peanutty goodness of this cold noodle salad really hits the spot. Creamy and tangy with just the right amount of kick from the ginger and chili paste, it's great as a side or main course. The peanut sauce is also tasty as salad dressing on greens for folks trying to cut out carbs, but we think that is decidedly less fun. "I love this sauce so much, I've even used it as a dipping sauce for baby carrots and as a salad dressing." —HILARY

1 pound spaghetti, angel hair pasta, or rice noodles

¾ cup creamy peanut butter (Skippy or Jiff works best)

⅓ cup rice vinegar (found in the international aisle of your market)

3 tablespoons soy sauce

4 teaspoons sambal oelek (Asian chili garlic sauce found in the international aisle of your market)

1½ teaspoons sesame oil (optional)

4 teaspoons fresh ginger, grated

zest and juice from 2 limes

¾ teaspoon kosher salt

¾ cup canola oil

½ cup fresh cilantro, roughly chopped

⅓ cup scallions (just the white parts), chopped

¼ cup salted peanuts, roughly chopped (optional)

1. Cook noodles according to package directions. Drain in a colander and rinse under cold water.

2. In a food processor, combine the peanut butter, vinegar, soy sauce, sambal oelek, sesame oil (if using), ginger, lime zest and juice, and salt. Pulse until all the ingredients are well incorporated. Turn machine ON and slowly add the canola oil through the small feed tube in a steady stream; don't overmix or the sauce will separate.

3. In a separate bowl, toss the pasta with peanut dressing and garnish with cilantro, scallions, and peanuts. Serve immediately or cover and refrigerate for up to 3 hours.

TRICK

Freeze your ginger ahead of time for easy grating. You can even leave the skin on.

TANDOORI SALMON SALAD

(GF)

Tandoori dishes get their name from the tandoor, a clay or metal oven fueled by a charcoal or wood fire that is used for cooking and baking in Southern, Central, and Western Asia. And while the oven heats food over a flame, the bright red color of the dish actually comes from the paprika and chili pepper in the sauce. This salmon salad is a play on the traditional flavors of the tandoor. It's yummy and light served warm or cold.

SALMON MARINADE

½ cup Greek yogurt

1 tablespoon cilantro, chopped

zest from 1 lemon plus juice from half of the lemon

1 clove garlic, grated

2 teaspoons fresh ginger, grated

1 teaspoon ground cumin

¾ teaspoon paprika

½ teaspoon turmeric

½ teaspoon chili powder

1 tablespoon tomato paste

1 tablespoon distilled white vinegar

salt and pepper to taste

4 filets (4-6 ounces each) salmon

DRESSING

½ cup mango chutney

¼ cup white wine vinegar

SALAD

10 ounces spring lettuce mix

½ red onion, sliced thin

2 tablespoons cilantro, chopped

1 cup cherry tomatoes, halved

1. Combine all ingredients, except the salmon, in a resealable plastic bag. Add the salmon and toss to coat. Place in the refrigerator and marinate for 30 minutes.

2. Turn your oven to a high broil. Line a rimmed cookie sheet with foil and spray with nonstick cooking spray.

3. Remove salmon from marinade and place on the prepared cookie sheet. Place pan in the oven 6 inches from the broiler and cook for 7-9 minutes until the salmon is light pink and cooked through.

4. In the food processor, puree the chutney and vinegar.

5. In a mixing bowl, combine the lettuce, onion, cilantro, and tomatoes, and toss with chutney vinegar dressing. Divide salad between 4 bowls and top with cooked salmon

TRICK

You can substitute chicken for the salmon. The dish is great cold, so make it the night before and serve it for lunch.

BACKYARD CITRUS CHICKEN

(GF)

"I'm a citrus freak. My first house had a lemon and orange tree in the backyard, and my neighbors had a lime tree that I would raid all the time. It only took a few extra ingredients to make this dish. It's one of my grilling staples. Tastes great on fish too!" —LOGAN

1½ pounds chicken breasts

zest and juice from 1 orange

zest and juice from 1 lemon

zest and juice from 1 lime

3 cloves garlic, roughly chopped

2 teaspoons fresh rosemary, roughly chopped

3 tablespoons extra-virgin olive oil

1 teaspoon salt

½ teaspoon pepper

1. Place all ingredients in a resealable plastic bag and marinate in the refrigerator for up to 2–4 hours. Do not marinate overnight, because the citrus will break down the protein.

2. Clean and oil the grill grates or grill pan and heat to a medium high heat (around 400°F). Take chicken out of marinade and place on grill for 5-7 minutes per side depending on the thickness, or until a thermometer reaches 160°F. Serve immediately.

TRICK

Cut the chicken breasts in half or pound the thick end of the chicken with a meat mallet to create a uniform thickness that will cook more evenly and quickly and will prevent the meat from drying out.

BUTTERCAKE BAKERY LEMON BARS

(V)

Citrus lovers will flip for Buttercake Bakery's signature Lemon Bars. The generous layer of tangy lemon curd on top of a flakey butter crust is the perfect balance of tart and sweet. It's impossible to eat just one. "These are my favorite! They are the easiest to make. I've tried hundreds of other recipes but nothing could compare."—LOGAN

CRUST

1½ sticks (6 ounces) unsalted butter, cold, plus extra to butter pan

1½ cups all-purpose flour

½ cup powdered sugar

FILLING

6 eggs, room temperature

3 cups granulated sugar

1 cup lemon juice

zest from 1 lemon

½ cup all-purpose flour

Powdered sugar for dusting

1. Preheat oven to 350°F. Butter a 9 x 13-inch pan.

2. To make the crust, combine flour, powdered sugar, and butter in a food processor and pulse until the mixture is the size of small peas.

3. Press dough into prepared pan. Bake for 15–20 minutes, until the crust is a pale, golden brown. Remove from the oven, let cool on a cooling rack and assemble the filling.

4. To make the filling, whisk together eggs and sugar in a small mixing bowl until well combined. Stir in lemon juice and zest. Add in the flour and stir until all the ingredients are well combined.

5. Pour lemon filling onto the pre-baked crust.

RECIPE CONTINUES ⟶

6. Transfer pan to oven and bake for 40 minutes, until the filling is set and slightly golden on top.

7. Remove bars from the oven and cool in the fridge to make them easier to slice.

8. Run a paring knife around the edge of the pan to release the bars and flip out onto a cutting board. Once removed, slice the bars into 2-inch squares. Fill a small sifter or mesh colander with a few tablespoons of powdered sugar and dust the top of the bars.

TRICK

For perfectly cut slices, pop the bars in the freezer for 15 minutes and then slice with a serrated knife.

CLASSIC CHOCOLATE PUDDING

(GF, V)

While researching the origin of Chocolate Pudding (because we love nerdy cooking trivia), we came across this tidbit from Wikipedia: "It was not considered a health food in the modern sense of the term, but as a wholesome, high-calorie food for those with poor appetites due to insanity at certain hours of the morning." So there you have it. Chocolate pudding is a cure for morning insanity. Have it for breakfast with coffee, and perhaps the rest of the day will be insanity-free. Or make it the day ahead and serve for dessert at a dinner party.

PUDDING

1½ cups + ½ cup milk, divided

½ cup granulated sugar

⅓ cup natural unsweetened cocoa powder (not hot chocolate mix)

4 teaspoons cornstarch

¼ teaspoon salt

3 egg yolks

2 teaspoons pure vanilla extract

WHIPPED CREAM AND TOPPING

1 cup heavy cream, chilled

1 tablespoon granulated sugar

½ teaspoon pure vanilla extract

favorite chocolate bar for shaving

1. In a saucepan over medium heat, combine 1½ cups milk, sugar, and cocoa until small bubbles form around the edge (do not let the mixture boil!), then remove from heat.

2. In a mixing bowl, whisk ½ cup milk, cornstarch, salt, yolks, and vanilla.

3. Slowly add the warm milk mixture from the saucepan to the egg mixture in the bowl. Use a whisk to combine.

4. Return the mixture to the saucepan and cook over medium heat until the pudding comes to full boil. Reduce the heat to low and cook until the mixture thickens, about 3 more minutes.

RECIPE CONTINUES ○——→

5. Pour pudding into 6 small glasses (any kind of vessel will work—coffee cups, ramekins; champagne or martini glasses are a nice, fancy touch.) Cover each serving with plastic wrap touching the top of each pudding so a skin does not form. Refrigerate for at least 4 hours, or overnight.

6. Before serving, make the whipped cream. In a stand mixer with the wire whip/whisk attachment, whip the cream, sugar, and vanilla on high (speed 6) until soft peaks form (peaks fall over when whip/whisk attachment is lifted). Spoon a dollop of whipped cream on top of each pudding serving and then use a zester/grater to shave the chocolate bar directly on top for presentation.

To add extra flair, alternate layers of pudding with dollops of whipped cream. Prepare the whipped cream at the same time as the pudding. In the serving glasses, add a layer of pudding , top it with cream, and repeat until the glass is full. Let set for at least 4 hours.

PANNA COTTA

(GF)

"I learned how to make Panna cotta at a cooking class in Positano, Italy. Panna cotta is Italian for 'cooked cream.' It's a great no-bake dessert, and I love that it can be made ahead of time. I serve these in cocktail glasses to dress them up." —LOGAN

¼ cup water

1 (¼-ounce) packet unflavored gelatin

4 cups heavy cream

1 cup granulated sugar

zest from 1 orange

1 teaspoon pure vanilla extract

2 cups fresh berries, as garnish

1. In a small mixing bowl, combine water and gelatin and let sit for 5 minutes. It will thicken and resemble clear jelly.

2. In a saucepan over medium heat, combine the cream, sugar, orange zest, and vanilla and bring to a simmer. You will see a few small bubbles around the edge, but don't let the mixture come to a boil.

3. Stir the mixture until the sugar has dissolved. Then remove the pan from the heat and add in the gelatin mixture. Stir to combine.

4. Divide the mixture between 6 serving glasses. Let the glasses cool slightly on the counter, and then cover in plastic wrap. Refrigerate for at least 6 hours, or overnight.

These can be made 3 days ahead of time and kept in the refrigerator. Serve chilled and top with fresh berries when ready to serve.

TRICK

Panna cotta is naturally gluten-free. You can also substitute coconut or almond milk and make this recipe dairy-free.

VELVET HAMMER SANGRIA

(V)

This recipe was contributed by guest chef, Liz Laffont.

"It was high summer and we had eaten tons of peaches from the tree in our yard. We were cobbled out but didn't want to waste the amazing fruit. So one afternoon, I stopped thinking desserts and invented this alternative version of classic sangria. Cheers!" —LIZ

3 bottles Riesling or other sweet wine

1 cup peach schnapps

juice and zest from 1 lemon

2 oranges, juice and zest from 1 orange, the other cut into half-round slices

¼ cup granulated sugar

2 teaspoons pure vanilla extract

3 peaches, pitted and cut into wedges

1 cup fresh raspberries

1. In a large pitcher combine all ingredients and chill 30 minutes to overnight. Serve over ice.

TRICK

If peaches aren't in season, use frozen peaches.

CHAPTER 5

LE CREUSET STOCKPOT FULL OF LOVE

RECIPES IN THIS CHAPTER

CORA'S SLICED SWEET PICKLES	150	CHICKEN AND CHORIZO PAELLA	164
COCONUT RICE	152	WINE-BRAISED BRISKET	166
PULLED PORK SANDWICHES	154	HALIBUT WITH COUSCOUS AND SUNDRIED TOMATOES	168
MEDITERRANEAN BEEF STEW	156		
MUSSELS WITH SAUSAGE	158	KETTLE CORN	170
TURKEY CHILI	160	DONUT HOLES	172
VEGETABLE COCONUT CURRY	162		

THE LE CREUSET STOCKPOT

Thanks to a universal love of pasta, hefty stockpots have been boiling up water for spaghetti since the dawn of noodles. Ranging in size from 1–13 quarts, sporting durable loop handles, and fashioned out of different metals, not all stockpots are created equal. For a pot to be truly versatile it should be made out of nonreactive metal. Ingredients like tomatoes, citrus, and wine are high in acidity and react when they come in contact with aluminum, copper, and non-enameled cast iron, causing the pans to stain or the finish to deteriorate, or even worse, give food a tinny taste. Stainless steel, anodized aluminum, and enameled cast iron are nonreactive.

If you truly want to just boil water for pasta, a lightweight, anodized aluminum pot will do just fine. But if you're interested in branching out and trying some of the recipes in this chapter, we recommend a heartier cast-iron pot. Made from molten iron poured into molds, cast-iron pots are a favorite amongst the pros and intrepid home cooks, because they possess the best heat distribution. They can go on the stovetop, into the oven, and last longer than most of us will be alive.

One of the hotly coveted "big ticket" cooking items is the Le Creuset enameled cast-iron Round French Oven—just ask any bride or groom armed with a registry scanner and a dream of becoming a gourmet cook. "Le creuset" is French for cauldron. We love that witchy vibe and think more people should refer to it as such, but it is more commonly called a dutch oven, stockpot, or casserole. Designed in vibrant fashion colors, these handsome pots look great sitting on a shelf but are also incredible workhorses. Iron cast and coated in a ceramic glaze to prevent food from taking on a metallic taste, the thick bottom conducts heat evenly and the tight fitting lid keeps all the moisture in the pot, where it belongs. French Ovens are famous for braising, slow cooking, and stewing but are capable of so much more.

A BIT OF HISTORY

In 1925, in a magical land called Fresnoy-le-Grand, Aisne, Picardy in France, two Belgian industrialists teamed up to open the Le Creuset foundry. Armand Desaegher was an expert in metal casting and Octave Aubecq, an enameling specialist. Together they produced the very first French Oven in bright orange or "volcanic flame," inspired by the color of molten iron inside of a cauldron. Over the years, the color palette expanded to reflect the fashionable hues of each decade. Today, the pots are available in a virtual rainbow of colors.

SO WHAT CAN IT DO? AND WHY DO YOU NEED IT?

A Le Creuset Round French Oven doesn't come cheap. At $369 for one $7 \frac{1}{4}$ quart pot, it costs more than an Artisan Series KitchenAid

Stand Mixer. Insert a frugal grandpa's voice here: "THREE HUNDRED AND SIXTY NINE DOLLARS FOR A COOKING POT? Is it made out of GOLD??" While the price might sound steep, it is absolutely worth it. First of all, the pots are still individually cast in sand molds and hand inspected by not one, not three, but fifteen skilled craftsmen. And boy, are they durable. They can be used on every heat source imaginable including gas, electric, induction, and vitro-ceramic. Heck, you can even thrust one into a campfire and it'll come out looking as pretty as when it went in. Speaking of pretty, these pots double as good-looking serving dishes. Pull one out of the oven and place it right on the table as the centerpiece of the meal—just make sure to put a trivet under it so you don't burn the table.

HERE'S A RECAP OF THE BENEFITS:

- Cast iron allows for the best heat induction and distribution.
- The shape is designed to accommodate larger and longer cuts of meat, and the broad bottom allows more room for an even cook.

- The tight-fitting lid keeps moisture from escaping.
- Enameled coating makes it easier to check browning and reduces stickiness for easy cleaning.
- Durable material means it can bake or roast in an oven or on the stovetop for hours, thus enhancing all the natural flavors of the food.
- It's perfect for one-pot meals. The French Oven has been cranking out one-pot meals long before a crockpot ever saw the light of day.
- The tall sides of the pot make it ideal for deep-frying or popping popcorn. Just to prove it, you'll find a recipe for Donut Holes (page 172) and Kettle Corn (page 170) in this chapter.

HOW TO USE YOUR LE CREUSET FRENCH OVEN/ STOCKPOT

You may feel like skipping this section because you already know how to use a darn pot! But there are some best practices for keeping your cast-iron cookware in good shape. It will only take a minute to read and might mean life or death for your expensive cookware.

1. Always preheat the pot first at a low temperature before you start cooking. This will ensure that the heat is evenly distributed throughout. Cover the entire cooking surface with oil, butter, or liquid to cook food evenly and avoid sticky messes.

2. Sprinkle some water from the tips of your fingers into the pan, and if it sizzles, the pan is ready for use.

3. Be mindful of the heat level. Too high, too quickly will cause the food to brown, burn, and stick to the bottom. Low to medium heats are best for frying and searing.

4. Never add cold liquid to a hot pot while cooking; the shock of the temperature change may cause the enamel to crack.

5. Use silicone, plastic, or wooden utensils to stir or flip food while cooking. Metal is safe to use, but over time it can scratch or damage the enamel coating. You may as well avoid it, because that pot is an investment.

6. It's safe to put your cast-iron pot into the oven, but check which version you have to determine the heat settings. The standard French Oven has a black phenolic knob that is safe in the oven up to 375°F. The Signature Range has composite knobs, and those can withstand heat up to 500°F. Stainless steel knobs are safe at any temperature.

HOW TO CLEAN IT

Make sure the pot is completely cool before attempting to clean it. Add warm, soapy water to the pot and clean with a nonabrasive sponge or brush. If some bits of food are stuck to the sides or bottom, let the pot soak for fifteen to twenty minutes with soapy water. These pots can also go in the dishwasher.

Now go ahead and work that pot!

CORA'S SLICED SWEET PICKLES

(GF, DF, V)

This recipe was contributed by guest chef Kristin Stark.

"I never really knew my great-grandmother, Cora, since she passed away when I was very young. I certainly got to know her better, though, through her recipes. For years I'd heard the stories from my mother and uncle about what a fantastic cook Cora was, and certainly no holiday meal was ever complete without her famous cranberry salad. After tasting some homemade pickles at a restaurant in New York a few summers ago, I was on a mission to learn how to make some for myself. I had tried my hand at dill and bread & butter, when my mom reminded me of Cora's sweet pickles, which were served at every big family dinner. They were so easy to make that I ended up canning gallons of them that summer to take back to Texas to share and enjoy with my mom and uncle!" —KRISTIN

4 cups sliced cucumbers, cut into ¼-inch-thick rounds (pickling cucumbers are great if you can find them)

¾ teaspoon salt

1½ cups distilled white vinegar, divided in half

¼ cup water

1½ cups + 2 tablespoons granulated sugar, divided

⅓ teaspoon celery seed

¼ teaspoon whole allspice

TRICK

Use a mandolin to make uniform slices, but wear a safety glove to protect your hand from that sharp blade!

1. In stockpot on medium heat, simmer cucumber slices, salt, ¾ cup vinegar, and water for 10 minutes. The bright green color of the cucumbers will fade.

2. Add 2 tablespoons sugar to the pot and let cook for an additional 2 minutes.

3. Drain the cucumbers in a colander and transfer them to a container with a lid (should hold 4 cups).

4. In the pot, combine ¾ cup vinegar, 1½ cups sugar, celery seed, and allspice and bring to a boil. Once the sugar has dissolved, pour mixture over cucumbers. Let cool slightly then cover with the lid and refrigerate.

5. Chill for at least 1 hour before serving. The pickles will be good for 5 days stored in the fridge.

COCONUT RICE

(GF, DF, V)

Toasted coconut adds so much flavor and texture to baked treats, why not add it to rice? Popular in pretty much every culture where coconut trees grow, this yummy rice is a standard side dish in Colombia, a dessert in Thailand, and an auspicious meal in special events in Sri Lanka. Feel free to serve it whenever the mood strikes you.

½ cup sweetened shredded coconut

1 tablespoon extra-virgin olive oil

2 cloves garlic, minced

¼ teaspoon red pepper chili flakes

1 cup basmati rice

1 cup chicken stock or vegetable stock

1 cup coconut milk

¼ cup cilantro, chopped

salt and pepper to taste

1. Add sweetened shredded coconut to a small sauté pan over low heat. Stir constantly for 4–5 minutes, until golden. Remove coconut from pan and set aside.

2. In a stockpot over medium heat, add olive oil.

3. When the oil is hot, add the garlic and the red pepper chili flakes. Sauté until soft and fragrant, 1–2 minutes.

4. Add the rice and stir to coat.

5. Add the stock and the coconut milk and bring to a boil.

6. Once the rice begins to boil, turn the heat to low. Place the lid on the pot and simmer for about 20 minutes, or until the rice is cooked and all the liquid has been absorbed.

7. Fluff rice with a fork and stir in the toasted coconut and cilantro. Season with salt and pepper to taste. Serve warm.

TRICK

Coconut can go from brown to burnt very fast so check it often while toasting.

PULLED PORK SANDWICHES

(DF)

"It was just a routine jaunt to the farmers market in Jackson, Wyoming, until my friend Liz and I stopped dead in our lettuce-hunting, tomato-grabbing tracks and discovered a vendor selling pulled pork sandwiches. Right before a planned dinner, when there was no reason to eat, we devoured the pork, mustard, and coleslaw combo. I spent the whole next day trying to recreate it and now you can see what the fuss was about." —LOGAN

PORK

3 pounds boneless pork shoulder
(Boston butt)

1 batch Dry Spice Rub (page 16)

3 yellow onions, cut into ¼-inch half-
rounds

1 bag of hamburger buns

Mustard Sauce

Creamy Coleslaw (page 64)

MUSTARD SAUCE

1 tablespoon extra-virgin olive oil

¼ cup yellow onion, minced

3 cloves garlic, chopped

1 cup yellow mustard

1 teaspoon dry mustard

½ cup ketchup

2 tablespoons granulated sugar

2 tablespoons packed brown sugar

1 teaspoon chili powder

1 tablespoon Worcestershire sauce

2 teaspoons red pepper flakes

¾ cup water

1. Preheat oven to 300°F. Use your fingers to cover the entire pork shoulder with Dry Spice Rub.

2. In a stockpot, place onion slices on the bottom and set the seasoned pork on top of the onions. Cover the pot and bake in the oven until the pork is very tender and can be easily shredded with a fork. This will take about 3 hours. Use tongs to flip the pork every hour to make sure it cooks evenly.

3. While the pork cooks, prepare the Mustard Sauce and Creamy Coleslaw (page 64). To make Mustard Sauce, sauté olive oil, onion, and garlic in a medium saucepan for 3 minutes over medium heat, or until fragrant. Add the rest of the ingredients and stir to combine, then turn heat to low and simmer for 20 minutes.

4. Once the pork has cooked, remove the pot from the oven. Take the pork out of the pot and transfer it to a plate and let it cool slightly. Using two forks or your hands, shred (or pull) all the meat into bite-size pieces. Add the shredded pork back to the pot and combine it with the onions and any liquids that accumulated during cooking.

5. To serve, pile shredded pork, mustard sauce, and creamy coleslaw onto the sliced buns.

MEDITERRANEAN BEEF STEW

(DF)

Mediterranean cuisine's signature flavors of citrus, wine, fresh herbs, olives, and tomatoes paired with cooked meats and seafood are derived from the native ingredients of the countries that border the Mediterranean Sea. The orange zest, tomatoes, and red wine in this stew enhance the taste of the beef for a one-pot feast that is sure to please. "Los Angeles isn't known for its harsh winters, so when it drops below 60°F, I can't wait to make this recipe and some Scallion Parmesan Drop Biscuits (page 70) to sop up the sauce." —LOGAN

4 pounds beef chuck roast, cut into 1½-inch cubes

salt and pepper to season beef

3 tablespoons extra-virgin olive oil

3 yellow onions, cut into ¼-inch half-rounds

1 can (6 ounces) tomato paste

6 cloves garlic, minced

1 tablespoon brown packed sugar

zest from ½ orange

2 teaspoons Herbes de Provence*

2 dried bay leaves

⅓ cup all-purpose flour

3 cups red wine (use a wine you would drink, since the flavor will concentrate)

1 cup chicken stock

¼ cup soy sauce

1½ pounds carrots, peeled, sliced, and cut into chunks

1 can (14.5 ounces) diced tomatoes, drained

....

Herbes de Provence is a mixture of dried herbs that include savory, marjoram, rosemary, thyme, oregano, and lavender. They are mostly herbs that are native to Provence, France, though the lavender was added for the American market.

1. Preheat oven to 325°F.

2. Season beef with salt and pepper and set aside.

3. In a stockpot over medium heat, add olive oil and onions and sauté for 5 minutes until the onions begin to soften.

4. Add the tomato paste, garlic, brown sugar, orange zest, Herbes de Provence, bay leaves, and flour to the pot. Cook this mixture for 1 minute over medium heat. Then add in the wine, stock, and soy sauce, cooking until the mixture starts to thicken, about 5 minutes.

5. Add the carrots and drained tomatoes. Place the seasoned beef on top of the sauce in the pan, so it can brown. Carefully transfer the uncovered pot to the oven.

6. Cook for approximately 2½–3 hours, until beef is tender, stirring the stew every hour. Serve warm.

MUSSELS WITH SAUSAGE

(GF, DF)

Mussels are rich in B12, an essential vitamin to keep the brain healthy. And if you're hosting a big dinner party, you need to stay on your toes. This quick recipe is a real dinner party showstopper. Tasty and hearty, it only takes about 30 minutes to make and looks as elegant and sophisticated as four-star restaurant fare.

1 pound spicy Italian sausages, casing removed

1 medium yellow onion, diced

3 cloves garlic, roughly chopped

1 can (14.5 ounces) crushed tomatoes

1 cup white wine (use a wine you would drink, since the flavor will concentrate)

½ cup chicken or fish stock

4 pounds mussels, cleaned and debearded (if you ask nicely, your fishmonger will do this step for you)

2 tablespoons extra-virgin olive oil

¼ cup fresh parsley, chopped, divided in half

salt and pepper to taste

a loaf of crusty bread

1. In a stockpot over medium heat, add the sausage. Break up the sausage as it browns.

2. Add the onions and garlic and cook until softened, but not browned, about 5 minutes.

3. Raise the temperature to high and add the tomatoes, wine, and broth. Bring to a boil for 2 minutes.

4. Reduce heat to medium and add in the mussels, stirring a few times to combine. Cover the pot with a lid and cook for 5 minutes.

5. With a slotted spoon remove mussels from the pot and transfer to the serving dish. Discard any mussels that did not open.

6. Add the olive oil and half the parsley into the pot with the cooking liquid and stir to combine. Let the sauce cook for 2 minutes. Season with salt and pepper.

7. Pour the sauce over the mussels and top with the remaining parsley. Serve immediately with crusty bread to sop up the extra sauce.

TRICK

Do steps 1–3 before your guests arrive. That way you can do a little chitchatting and dash back to the kitchen to bring the sauce to a boil and add in the mussels. Before anyone realizes you're gone, dinner will be ready to serve!

TURKEY CHILI

(GF, DF)

In the dead of winter, nothing warms your insides like a steaming pot of chili. Our turkey version is a low-fat, healthy alternative with a great kick from the chipotle peppers in adobo sauce. Chipotles in adobo are dried jalapeño peppers with a rich, smoky flavor that have been canned in a red, tomato-based sauce. They are spicy, but if used in small amounts, they can turn up the flavor in a dish without making your eyes burn. Serve with a batch of your favorite cornbread.

1 medium yellow onion, diced

2 carrots, peeled and diced

2 stalks of celery, diced

1 red bell pepper, diced

3 cloves garlic, roughly chopped

2 chipotle peppers in adobo (found in the international aisle of your market)

2 tablespoons extra-virgin olive oil

1¼ pounds ground turkey, preferably dark meat

3 tablespoons chili powder

1½ teaspoons garlic powder

1½ teaspoons dried oregano

1½ teaspoons ground cumin

½ teaspoon dried thyme

½ teaspoon red pepper flakes

¼ cup packed brown sugar

1 tablespoon salt

2 teaspoons pepper

3 tablespoons tomato paste

1 can (28 ounces) diced tomatoes

2 cups chicken stock

TRICK

It's a huge time saver to use the food processor to dice the veggies but be sure to cut the veggies into big chunks before you toss them in to ensure that all the pieces end up about the same size.

1. In a food processor, dice the onion, carrots, celery, bell pepper, garlic, and chipotle peppers by pulsing 20–30 times until everything is chopped into small pieces. You can also slice everything by hand with a chef's knife.

2. In a stockpot over medium heat, add the olive oil and sauté the onion, carrots, celery, bell pepper, garlic, and chipotle peppers until tender. This will take about 8 minutes.

3. Add the ground turkey to the pot, breaking it up into chunks with a wooden spoon, and cook until it's no longer pink. Add in chili powder, garlic powder, oregano, cumin, thyme, red pepper flakes, brown sugar, salt, and pepper, and cook for 2 minutes.

4. Add the tomato paste, diced tomatoes, and stock into the pot. On medium heat, bring the chili to a boil. Then reduce heat to low and simmer for 30 minutes. Serve hot. This can also be made the day before and reheated.

VEGETABLE COCONUT CURRY

(GF, DF, V)

A curry is a dish or a sauce, often made with coconut milk and robust spices, influenced by Indian cooking. It is not to be confused with curry powder, a seasoning made from a mixture of several fragrant spices, including turmeric, coriander, and cumin, with a pungent flavor that marries well with beef, fish, poultry, and vegetables. This veggie curry is a hearty one-pot meal for the whole family. Filling and tasty, we guarantee people will make a return trip to the stockpot.

2 tablespoons extra-virgin olive oil

1 medium yellow onion, cut into ¼-inch half-rounds

4 cloves garlic, minced

2 tablespoons ginger, grated

1 zucchini, halved and chopped

1 cup cauliflower (about ¼ of a head), cut into florets

1 bell pepper, large dice

1 sweet potato, peeled and diced

1 can (15 ounces) chickpeas, drained and rinsed

1 can (12 ounces) coconut milk

1 cup vegetable stock

2 tablespoons packed brown sugar

1 tablespoon curry powder

¼–¾ teaspoon cayenne pepper (depending on how hot you like it)

salt and pepper to taste

3 cups of cooked rice

1. In a stockpot over medium heat, heat olive oil. Next, add onion, garlic, and ginger. Sauté for 2 minutes, just until fragrant.

2. Add in the zucchini, cauliflower, bell pepper, sweet potato, chickpeas, coconut milk, vegetable stock, brown sugar, curry powder, cayenne pepper, and bring to a boil.

3. Cover pot, reduce heat to low, and simmer for 20 minutes. Season with salt and pepper. Serve over rice.

TRICK

Swap in your favorite veggies; we suggest alternatives like spinach, green beans, tomatoes, broccoli, or carrots. Cut vegetables should total 4 cups.

CHICKEN and CHORIZO PAELLA

(GF, DF)

Paella pronounced pah-EH-ya, is a delicious Valencian rice dish made with seafood and/or meat. It originated in the nineteenth century on the eastern coast of Spain. The dish derives its signature yellow hue from saffron, one of the world's most expensive spices, due to the fact that it requires the harvest of 50,000–75,000 crocus flowers to yield 1 pound of dry saffron. In this recipe, we decided to save you a few bucks and substituted the saffron with turmeric for flavor and paprika for color. This is a truly delectable one-pot meal. You're welcome.

2 tablespoons extra-virgin olive oil

1 pound chicken breasts, cut into ½-inch cubes

salt and pepper to season chicken

½ pound cured chorizo, cut into ¼-inch slices (if using fresh chorizo, remove the casings)

1 medium yellow onion, diced

1 bell pepper, diced

1½ cups Arborio rice

2 cloves garlic, chopped

½ teaspoon ground turmeric

1 teaspoon paprika

1 teaspoon dried oregano

1 dried bay leaf

¼ teaspoon red pepper chili flakes

1 can (14.5 ounces) diced tomatoes, drained

½ teaspoon salt

¼ teaspoon pepper

3 cups chicken stock

½ cup frozen peas

1 lemon, cut into wedges

1. Heat olive oil in a stockpot over medium heat.

2. Season the diced chicken with salt and pepper and place it into the pot. Brown the chicken on all sides (it doesn't need to fully cook now). Once browned, remove the chicken, transfer to a plate, and set aside.

3. Add the chorizo to the pot and cook until it begins to brown.

4. Add onion and bell pepper to the pot and cook until softened, about 3 minutes.

5. Add rice and garlic and stir with a wooden spoon for 1 minute to allow the rice to absorb all the flavors.

6. Add turmeric, paprika, oregano, bay leaf, red pepper chili flakes, drained tomatoes, salt, pepper, and stock to the pot.

7. Bring to a boil over medium heat, then reduce heat to low. Place the lid on the pot and cook for 15 minutes until most of the liquid has been absorbed.

8. Add the chicken, along with any juices that have accumulated from the meat, back into the pot and stir in the peas. Cook for an additional 5 minutes with the lid on, until rice is completely cooked. Serve hot with lemon wedges.

TRICK

Switch up the protein. Try adding in ½ pound of peeled and deveined shrimp for the last 5 minutes of cooking.

WINE-BRAISED BRISKET

(DF)

Brisket, the cut of beef or veal from the breast or lower chest, is probably best known as braised beef, a dish served at Jewish holiday celebrations. "My mom never makes her brisket the same way twice. So for the sake of having a Rosh Hashanah recipe to pass on, I have written it down for preservation." —LOGAN

2 medium yellow onions, sliced into ¼-inch half-rounds

4 cloves garlic, chopped

2 cups red wine (use a wine you would drink since the flavor will concentrate)

1 cup chicken or beef stock

3 tablespoons balsamic vinegar

2 tablespoons packed brown sugar

2 tablespoons tomato paste

1 can (14.5 ounces) diced tomatoes

1 teaspoon dried thyme

2 dried bay leaves

2 teaspoons salt

1 teaspoon pepper

1 first cut brisket* (about 5 pounds), trimmed of excess fat

Ask the butcher for "first cut" or "flat cut," which is the most lean meat from the pectoral muscle of the beef.

1. Preheat oven to 300°F.

2. Place all ingredients except the brisket in a stockpot. Then rest the brisket on top of all other ingredients. Note: The brisket will shrink during cooking.

3. Transfer to the oven and cook uncovered for 2 hours. Using tongs, flip the meat over and cook for an additional 1–1½ hours until the meat is very tender.

4. Remove pot from oven and let the brisket cool in the sauce for 30 minutes. Skim off any fat from sauce.

5. Transfer meat to a cutting board and, using a chef's knife, cut ½-inch slices across the grain. Serve with the sauce from the pot.

TRICK

Properly cutting beef can be the difference between tough and tender. Determine the direction of the grain (muscle fibers) on the meat. They will run in the same direction down the length of meat. Hold your knife crosswise to the grain and then cut thin slices of meat. When you cut against the grain, you get hundreds of tiny fibers instead of one long one, and it makes the meat melt in your mouth. This is especially important when cutting brisket, flank, hanger, or skirt steaks.

HALIBUT WITH COUSCOUS *and* SUNDRIED TOMATOES

(GF, DF)

This healthy and flavorful halibut has the perfect balance of sweet accents from the sundried tomatoes and briny, tangy notes from the olives and capers. The texture of the couscous provides a lovely contrast to the other ingredients. Cooked in just one pot, it's super easy to make and just as easy to clean up.

⅓ cup oil-packed sundried tomatoes, chopped

2 tablespoons of the oil from the sundried tomatoes (or olive oil)

¼ cup kalamata olives, chopped

1 tablespoon capers, drained

½ teaspoon dried thyme

2 cloves garlic, chopped

zest from 1 lemon

1 tablespoon balsamic vinegar

½ cup uncooked couscous

½ cup broth (chicken or vegetable)

2 halibut fillets (4–6 ounces each)

1. Preheat oven to 400°F.

2. Coat the inside of a stockpot liberally with nonstick cooking spray.

3. In a small mixing bowl, combine the sundried tomatoes, sundried tomato oil, kalamata olives, capers, thyme, garlic, lemon zest, and balsamic vinegar.

4. Pour the couscous and broth into the bottom of the pot and mix. Lay the halibut on top of the couscous, and then spoon the tomato mixture on top of the fish.

5. Put the lid on the stockpot and place it in the oven. Bake for 15 minutes, until the fish is cooked to your liking.

TRICK

Feel free to substitute salmon, cod, sole, or even chicken.

KETTLE CORN

(GF, DF, V)

"DISCLAIMER: This Kettle Corn is like Kryptonite. You will be powerless against its addictive flavor. I have tried to eat only one handful, and I have failed, miserably. Easy to make but impossible to resist, put a bowl aside for yourself, and everyone else can share the rest. #Winning!"
—HILARY

3 tablespoons vegetable oil

½ cup popcorn kernels

½ teaspoon salt

½ cup powdered sugar

1 tablespoon granulated sugar

1 tablespoon packed brown sugar

1. In the stockpot, heat oil on high until ripples appear (but not smoke).

2. Add the kernels and salt and stir with a wooden spoon. Cover the pot with the lid, leaving it slightly ajar for steam to escape.

3. Combine the 3 sugars in a small bowl and set aside.

4. Once the kernels start popping, turn the heat down to medium.

5. When the popping slows down (about 2-3 seconds between pops), remove the pot from the flame and sprinkle the sugar mixture on top of the kernels.

6. Immediately place the pot back on a low flame and stir with a wooden spoon to distribute and melt the sugars for 30–60 seconds, until you see the sugars caramelizing on the bottom of the pot. Stir to coat the popcorn and then immediately transfer to a serving bowl and enjoy!

TRICK

Hand out packaged Kettle Corn as party favors or a homemade holiday gift. Scoop portions into cellophane bags and tie with a ribbon. Affix a little handwritten label to the front: "From the Kitchen of [your name]."

DONUT HOLES

(v)

All hail the donut! There are few foods that incite more glee than donuts. Now it's not 100 percent confirmed, but donuts appear to be one of the few foods that originated right here in the old US of A. We feel very proud of that accomplishment. Our homemade donut holes are a snap to make and crazy addictive, especially when they're still warm.

BATTER

canola oil for frying

1¼ cups all-purpose flour

2 teaspoons baking powder

¼ teaspoon salt

¼ cup granulated sugar

½ cup whole milk

3 tablespoons

unsalted butter, melted and cooled slightly

½ teaspoon pure vanilla extract

CINNAMON SUGAR TOPPING

½ cup granulated sugar

1 teaspoon ground cinnamon

TRICK ★

Heat the oil first. It will take longer to get the oil up to temperature than to make the batter. Want to know if your oil is hot enough for frying? Stick a wooden skewer or spoon in the oil. If bubbles form around the wood, then you are good to go.

1. In a 6- to 8-quart stockpot, add 1 inch of oil. Heat oil to 350°F.

2. In a mixing bowl, combine flour, baking powder, salt, and sugar. Make a well in the center and pour in the milk, melted butter, and vanilla. Stir until combined, but do not over mix.

3. Clip a candy thermometer to the side of the pot. Once the oil is heated to 350°F, use a small ice cream scoop and drop 6 balls into the oil at a time.

4. Fry for 3-4 minutes total, flipping once with a pair of tongs. It's time to flip when the dough in the oil is golden brown.

5. Remove the balls from the oil and drain off excess oil on paper towels.

6. In a bowl or paper bag mix the cinnamon and sugar. Add in the hot donuts and toss to coat. If using a paper bag, fold over the top of the bag and give the donuts a little shake to coat completely. Serve immediately.

CHAPTER 6

KITCHENAID TO THE RESCUE

RECIPES IN THIS CHAPTER

BUTTERCAKE BAKERY COFFEE CAKE   184

BUTTERCAKE BAKERY BANANA CAKE   187

BUTTERCAKE BAKERY BLUEBERRY CAKE   190

BUTTERCAKE BAKERY CHOCOLATE CAKE   192

BUTTERCAKE BAKERY
BUTTERCREAM FROSTING   195

BUTTERCAKE BAKERY
DARK CHOCOLATE FROSTING   196

LINDA'S CHOCOLATE CHIP COOKIE PIE   198

BUTTERCAKE BAKERY PECAN SNOWBALLS   201

CITRUS ALMOND CAKE   204

BUTTERCAKE BAKERY PUMPKIN WHOOPIE
PIES   207

BUTTERCAKE BAKERY CHEESECAKE   210

BROWN SUGAR MERINGUE BERRY STACK   213

ROSEMARY SEA SALT FOCACCIA   216

THE KITCHENAID STAND MIXER

Baking, with its tantalizing by-products of batter-coated bowls and delicious baked treats, tends to be the gateway drug that lures budding chefs into the kitchen. But baking is considered trickier than good old-fashioned cooking. There is very little winging it. Measurements must be exact, oven temperatures accurate, batter consistency just so. For those of us who have experienced mishaps, there is nothing sadder than too little frosting to cover the cake (oh yes, this happens), cookies with scorched bottoms, and fallen soufflés. Luckily, help is on the way. And when we say help, we're referring to Logan's Baking Decoded tips and a KitchenAid stand mixer.

Hand mixers are fine for boxed cake and pancake batters, but when it comes to tougher jobs like cookie doughs, pie crusts, and breads, there are many benefits to investing in a KitchenAid stand mixer.

The KitchenAid stand mixer comes equipped with a flat beater, dough hook, and wire whip that allows you to mix, knead, and whip your way to baking perfection. Constructed in heavy metal so that it stays in place during use, even when mixing heavy dough, it also gives your wrist a break from all that repetitive stirring. Say goodbye to carpal tunnel, because the KitchenAid's "planetary mixing action" (your batter is the sun and the rotating attachments are the planets) makes the beater, dough hook, or wire whip/whisk attachment spiral around the bowl so that the ingredients are mixed evenly. And while it rotates, it's covering sixty-seven points of the bowl per cycle. This is extremely important because evenly mixed ingredients are key to good baking results. It's a lot more work to get the same results with a hand mixer and a free-standing bowl that isn't clamped into place. You and the bowl will bounce along the counter when mixing heavier doughs.

A BIT OF HISTORY

Inventor Herbert Johnson watched a baker laboriously stir dough by hand with a spoon and knew there had to be a better way. He started working on an industrial electric mixer that would give bakers' tired arms a much-needed break. The first commercial electric stand mixer debuted in 1908 with an 80-quart capacity bowl and was sold by Hobart Manufacturing. In 1919, Troy Metal Products, a subsidiary of Hobart, released a scaled down stand mixer for professional counter tops. The very first model weighed sixty-nine pounds, and you pretty much had to be a bodybuilder to lug the thing around. The next iteration was much smaller and designed for home cooks. The company recruited Troy executives' wives to test the machine and see what it could do. Legend has it that as part of the focus group, they asked the women to come up with names for the machine. One of the gals said, "I don't care what you call it, but I know it's the best kitchen aid I have ever had." And voilà, the KitchenAid was born.

SO WHAT CAN IT DO AND WHY DO YOU NEED IT?

Available with bowls that can hold up to 8 quarts, the most popular KitchenAid is the Artisan Series priced at $250, which comes with a 5-quart bowl and a 325-watt motor. Don't hesitate to invite over a small army for dinner, because that 5-quart stainless steel bowl is big enough to mix dough for 4 loaves of bread or 7 pounds of mashed potatoes in a single batch. And the bowl is dishwasher safe for quick cleanup. But wait—there's more. The KitchenAid is like a Transformer; it's designed to easily convert into a pasta maker, a meat grinder, and even an ice cream maker with additional parts that fit into the attachment hub (all sold separately, of course). Visit the manufacturer's site to check out all the ways your machine can take on a new identity.

ARTISAN MODEL KITCHENAID

Parts and Features

1. TILT-BACK MOTOR HEAD WITH DIRECT DRIVE MOTOR: For tilt-head models (pictured), always tilt back the motor head when adding ingredients to clear more room over the bowl. When you're ready to mix, switch the motor head to the locked position by pushing the lock button into place on the right side of the machine. For bowl-lift models, rotate the lever to the up position. Bowl must always be lifted before mixing.

2. ATTACHMENT HUB: This magical hub allows you to transform your stand mixer into a pasta maker, meat grinder, and ice cream maker among other amazing things. Loosen the attachment hub by screwing it counterclockwise and remove the attachment hub cover, or flip up the hinged hub cover. Insert the attachment shaft housing into the attachment hub. Make sure the attachment power shaft fits into the square attachment hub socket. It may be necessary to rotate the attachment back and forth. When the attachment is in proper position, the pin on the attachment will fit into the notch on the hub rim.

3. FLAT BEATER: Use this guy for normal to heavy mixtures like cakes, creamed frostings, candies, cookies, pie pastry, biscuits, quick breads, meat loaf, and mashed potatoes.

4. 5-QUART STAINLESS STEEL MIXING BOWL WITH HANDLE: Big enough to mix dough for 9 dozen cookies. It can also beat as little as 1 egg white or up to 14 egg whites in a single batch

5. BOWL CLAMPING PLATE/BOWL SUPPORT: For tilt-head models (pictured), place the mixing bowl on the clamping plate to attach and turn it clockwise. Turn it counterclockwise to remove. For bowl-lift models, place the bowl lever in the down position. Fit bowl supports over the pins until it snaps into place.

6. DOUGH HOOK: Use the dough hook when mixing and kneading yeast doughs for breads, rolls, and buns.

7. WIRE WHIP/WHISK: This attachment is best for mixtures that need to incorporate air like eggs, egg whites, heavy cream, boiled frostings, sponge cakes, angel food cakes, and some candies.

8. SPEED CONTROL KNOB: This knob is used to adjust the speed of the attachments. Reference the speed chart to determine the correct settings for your recipe.

9. BEATER SHAFT: Attach flat beater, wire whip/whisk, and dough hook onto the beater shaft by pushing up and turning attachment like a light bulb.

SHIELD GUARD/SPLATTER GUARD: The shield guard fits right over the top of the bowl and prevents ingredients from flying all over the place. Rotate it so the motor head covers the U-shaped gap in the shield. The pouring chute will be just to the right of the attachment hub as you face the mixer. (Not pictured.)

HOW TO USE YOUR KITCHENAID STAND MIXER

The first thing you want to do is make sure the machine is unplugged. Depending on the model of your machine, either tilt the motor head back, and place the bowl on the bowl clamping plate turning the bowl clockwise until it tightens, or attach the bowl to holder pins and snap into place. Choose an attachment and push it up on the beater shaft, turning it like a light bulb until it locks in place. Newer KitchenAid mixers come with a pouring shield that helps guide the ingredients neatly into the bowl so you don't end up covered in flour. Set the shield right over the top of the bowl and rotate the shield so the motor head covers the U-shaped gap in the shield. The pouring chute will be just to the right of the attachment hub as you face the mixer. Lock the motor head down by pushing the lock lever (on the right hand side of the motor head) into place, which keeps the beaters steady during the mixing process. Once you've added your ingredients, plug in the mixer and choose your blending speed. It's best to start out on lower speeds and gradually work your way up; that way ingredients don't go flying all over the place. We've provided a speed guide below to help you determine exactly which level is best for your recipe. You don't want to scrape the bowl while the stand mixer is running because you might catch a spatula in the beater and jam up the works. Occasional scraping is important to incorporate ingredients—just turn off the stand mixer first. The machine may warm up during use. This is normal, so don't panic and think it's going to explode; it won't.

HOW TO CLEAN YOUR KITCHENAID STAND MIXER

Wipe the base clean with a wet dishtowel. Avoid using toxic cleansers that you wouldn't want near food, and never immerse the base in water. The metal bowl, white-coated flat beater, and white-coated dough hook may be washed in a dishwasher. If you don't have a dishwasher, clean each part thoroughly in hot sudsy water and rinse completely before drying. The metal wire whip/whisk, burnished metal dough hook, and burnished metal flat beater should be hand washed only and dried immediately. Do not store the beaters on the shaft, because the KitchenAid manual says not to and that's good enough for us!

STIR – For slow stirring, combining, and beginning all mixing procedures. Use the STIR speed to add flour and dry ingredients to batter, flour to butter and sugar, liquids to dry ingredients, and combine heavy mixtures. It's a good speed for mixing muffin dough. Use this speed with the ice cream maker attachment.

SPEED 2 – For slow mixing, stirring, mashing, and faster stirring. Best to mix heavy batters and candies, start mashing potatoes or other vegetables, cut shortening into flour, mix thin or splashy batters, mix and knead yeast dough, and make pasta dough. Only use speed 2 when preparing yeast dough—using any other speed for bread dough may damage the mixer. Use this speed with the can opener attachment.

SPEED 4 – For mixing and beating semi-heavy batters, such as cookies. Best for combining sugar and shortening and adding sugar to egg whites for meringues. It's a good medium speed for cake mixes. Use with the food grinder, rotor slicer/shredder, and fruit/vegetable strainer attachments.

SPEED 6 – For medium-fast beating, creaming, and whipping. Use to finish mixing cake, donut, and other thinner batters. Can be used as a high speed for cake mixes. Use with the citrus juicer attachment.

SPEED 8 – For fast beating and whipping cream, egg whites, and boiled frostings.

SPEED 10 – For fast whipping small amounts of cream or egg whites. Use with the pasta maker and grain mill attachments.

NOTE: The speed control lever can be set between the speeds listed in the above chart to obtain speeds 3, 5, 7, and 9 if a finer adjustment is required.

BAKING DECODED CHECKLIST

1. Make sure you read the recipe all the way through before you start. Measure out all the ingredients and place everything on the counter before you begin. You don't want to discover that you don't have enough flour right when it's supposed to be added to the batter.

2. Always preheat your oven for at least 20 minutes before you bake.

3. Butter, milk, and eggs (and any other refrigerated ingredients) should be at room temperature. Remove from fridge 60 minutes prior to using. You can also cut butter into cubes to speed up the softening process and place cold eggs in a bowl of lukewarm water.

4. When baking, always use large Grade A eggs. Eggs separate easier when cold, but the whites whip up best at room temperature.

5. Make sure you measure ingredients with the right tools. Liquids should be measured in a glass liquid measuring cup set on a level counter. Spoon dry ingredients into correct-sized metal or plastic graduated measuring cups until they are overflowing. Then level them off with the back of a knife. When ingredients are listed in pounds, grams, or ounces, use a kitchen scale to determine accurate portions.

6. Many recipes require you to cream the butter and sugar. This is done to create small air pockets in the dough that will mix with the baking soda or baking powder and help baked goods to rise. Perfectly creamed butter and sugar should be pale yellow and fluffy; this will take about 5 minutes on medium (speed 4). If the butter starts to separate, you have over mixed and should start over.

7. Start and end with dry ingredients. Alternate in dry, wet, dry, wet, dry, wet, dry. This is done to cut down on gluten development, which makes the end product tough. By ending on dry ingredients like flour, the wetness of the batter is absorbed and ensures that all the ingredients are well combined. Don't overmix the batter once the dry ingredients are added in. Make sure to combine dry ingredients on a low speed so flour doesn't fly all over the place.

8. Regularly scrape down the sides and bottom of your mixing bowl with a spatula to make sure all ingredients are well incorporated.

9. If you don't have a rolling pin, you can use a bottle of wine. Just clean off the outside and remove the label so you have a clean surface to press against the dough.

10. To recover a piece of broken eggshell from your mixing bowl, use an empty half eggshell to retrieve it. Eggshells stick to eggshells.

11. Butter and flour your cake pans to prevent sticking. Make sure your pans are clean and dry. Take about 1 tablespoon butter and drop it into the pan. Use a folded paper towel or butter wrapper to rub the butter

all over the bottom and sides of the pan so that every inch is thinly coated. Next sprinkle about 1 tablespoon flour into the pan. Over a sink, shake the flour back and forth across the bottom and sides so the entire pan is coated. Shake out leftover flour into the sink.

12. Line springform pans with parchment to remove cakes more easily. Place your round pan on a piece of parchment paper and trace the bottom with a pen. Use scissors or an X-Acto knife to cut out the circle on the inside line and it will fit perfectly in your pan.

13. Never fill pans for cakes or cupcakes more than ¾ full or they may overflow during baking.

14. Don't overcrowd the oven. Always position pans in the center of your oven, never touching other pans or sides of the oven (try to leave at least 2 inches on all sides). If the oven is not wide enough to place pans side-by-side, stagger them on different racks slightly offset to allow circulation.

15. Rotate pans ⅔ of the way through the baking time. This will ensure even baking. If pans are on different racks, this is the time to swap the position of the pans and turn them front to back.

16. Let cakes sit for 5 minutes on a cooling rack before removing them from the pans and placing the cake directly on a rack to cool completely.

17. To test for doneness, use a toothpick and insert it into the center of the baked good. If it comes out with no crumbs stuck to the toothpick, it's done. Cakes will also start to pull away from the sides of the pan when they are done. Cakes and cupcakes should spring back when lightly touched.

18. Use timers! A few minutes too long can dry out baked goods. If given approximate baking times (5–8 minutes) check for doneness at the minimum time.

19. When frosting cakes, use a warm offset spatula (a long and narrow spatula with a thin, flat metal blade or paddle on one end) to smooth out frosting as you go. Begin by applying a "crumb coat" to minimize crumbs in the icing. Frost a completely cool cake with a thin layer and refrigerate the cake for 30 minutes. Refrost the cake over the crumb coat and decorate.

20. Gluten-free flour works well as a substitute in some recipes but not all. The one we have had the most success with is King Arthur's Gluten-Free Multi-Purpose Flour. You should experiment and see which recipes work best with substitutions.

21. If using glass or dark metal pans, reduce oven temperature by 25°F. If baking at high altitude (above 3,500 feet), raise the temperature by 25°F.

22. If you run out of powdered sugar, you can make your own if you have granulated sugar, cornstarch, and a clean coffee grinder or blender. Combine 1 cup granulated sugar and a 1 teaspoon cornstarch and let it spin for 30 seconds. Like magic—insta-powdered sugar.

23. When brown sugar has hardened into a brick, seal it in a plastic bag with a slice of bread for a few hours. The bread will release moisture into the granules, allowing them to separate so they are scoopable. This trick works to soften vanilla beans, too.

24. When a recipe calls for zest, instead of grating it into a separate container or onto parchment paper, hold the zester over the mixing bowl and zest directly onto the butter or cream. The aromatic citrus oils that are sprayed into the bowl will give the dessert a zingy finish.

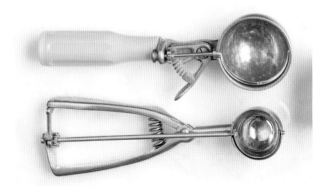

BUTTERCAKE BAKERY COFFEE CAKE

(V)

Nothing tastes better with a cup of coffee than cinnamony, nutty coffee cake. On weekends at Buttercake Bakery, customers would call ahead to find out when this cake was coming out of the oven and line up outside waiting for their fix. WARNING: If you bake this at home, your friends and family might form a queue next to your oven.

CINNAMON LAYER

½ cup granulated sugar

½ cup walnuts, chopped

1 tablespoon ground cinnamon

BATTER

1 stick (4 ounces) unsalted butter, room temperature

1 cup granulated sugar

2 eggs, room temperature

1 tablespoon lemon juice

1 teaspoon pure vanilla extract

2 cups all-purpose flour

½ teaspoon baking powder

1 teaspoon baking soda

½ teaspoon salt

1 cup sour cream, room temperature

1. Preheat oven to 325°F. Butter and flour a 9-inch bundt pan.

2. In a mixing bowl, mix the cinnamon layer ingredients together and set aside.

3. In a stand mixer, cream the butter and sugar on low (speed 2) and gradually increase speed to medium (speed 4) until mixture is pale and fluffy. This should take about 5 minutes.

4. Add the eggs, lemon juice, and vanilla into the mixer. Use a spatula to scrape down the sides and the bottom of the bowl and combine on medium (speed 4).

5. In a separate mixing bowl, combine the dry ingredients for the batter: flour, baking powder, baking soda, and salt.

RECIPE CONTINUES ○——→

6. With the mixer on medium speed (speed 4) alternate adding the dry ingredients and the sour cream into the mixer in several batches (dry, wet, dry, wet, dry). Use a spatula to scrape the sides and bottom of the bowl after each addition.

7. Spread ⅓ of the batter on the bottom of the prepared pan. Top the batter by sprinkling ⅓ of cinnamon layer. Repeat this procedure 2 more times, ending on cinnamon sugar.

8. Bake for 50 minutes or until a toothpick comes out dry. Remove the cake from the oven, and let it stand in the pan for 5 minutes before removing and placing it on a rack to cool. Serve warm or room temperature.

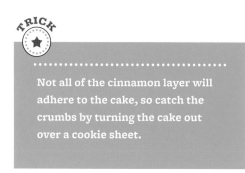

TRICK

Not all of the cinnamon layer will adhere to the cake, so catch the crumbs by turning the cake out over a cookie sheet.

BUTTERCAKE BAKERY BANANA CAKE

(V)

"I have flown this cake across the country for pregnancy cravings and turned it into birthday cakes, wedding cakes, and even an, 'I'm sorry I hit your parked car' cake. It's super yummy on its own, but feel free to add frosting or chocolate chips to make it a bit more decadent. This recipe makes 2 loaves. Eat one now and pop the second one in the freezer for a last minute brunch or tea time treat." —LOGAN

2 sticks (8 ounces) unsalted butter, room temperature

2½ cups granulated sugar

2 teaspoons pure vanilla extract

4 eggs, room temperature

½ cup sour cream, room temperature

2 teaspoons baking soda

3 cups all-purpose flour

½ teaspoon salt

1 pound (about 4 medium) ripe bananas (should have some brown spots on the peels), peeled and mashed with a fork

TRICK

If your bananas aren't quite soft enough or not yellow enough, place whole bananas on a cookie sheet in the oven on 200°F and bake them for 15 minutes. The skin will turn black and the fruit will become much sweeter because the heat draws out the sugar.

1. Preheat oven to 350°F. Butter and flour the 2 loaf pans and set aside.

2. In the bowl of a stand mixer, cream the butter and sugar starting on low (speed 2) and gradually increase speed to medium (speed 4) until mixture is pale and fluffy.

3. With the mixer speed on low (speed 2), add vanilla and the eggs, one at a time. After each addition, use a spatula to scrape down the sides and bottom of the bowl to make sure everything is well combined.

4. In a separate bowl or measuring cup, combine the sour cream and baking soda. With the mixer on low speed (speed 2), add sour cream and baking soda mixture.

RECIPE CONTINUES ⟶

5. On STIR speed, alternate the flour, salt, and bananas in 2 additions. Use a spatula to scrape down the sides and bottom of bowl after each addition.

6. Divide the batter evenly between the two prepared pans. Bake for 30 minutes and open the oven and rotate the pans (turning them 180 degrees) to ensure even baking results. Bake for another 20 minutes or until a toothpick comes out clean.

7. Let cakes cool in the pans for 5 minutes on a cooling rack, then remove the loaves and let cool completely on the racks.

8. You can frost the top of the cake with the Buttercake Bakery Buttercream Frosting (page 195), but these cakes are delicious naked, too.

BUTTERCAKE BAKERY BLUEBERRY CAKE

(V)

"What do you do when you're vacationing on a farm in the Hudson Valley with friends, drinking a glass of rosé, and have no dessert planned? Run to the backyard, pick blueberries, and reinvent a classic. The cream cheese keeps this cake super moist. It was such a big hit, I added it to the bakery menu when I got back to town." —LOGAN

CAKE

2 sticks (8 ounces) unsalted butter, room temperature

1½ cups granulated sugar

1 package (8 ounces) cream cheese, room temperature

2 eggs, room temperature

1 teaspoon pure vanilla extract

2 tablespoons lemon juice

1¾ cups all-purpose flour

1½ teaspoons baking powder

¼ teaspoon salt

1½ cups + ½ cup blueberries, divided

GLAZE

2 cups powdered sugar

zest from 1 lemon

3-4 tablespoons lemon juice (depending on your thickness preference)

1. Preheat oven to 350°F. Grease and flour a 9-inch bundt pan.

2. In the bowl of a stand mixer, cream the butter, sugar, and cream cheese on low (speed 2) and gradually increase speed to medium (speed 4) until mixture is pale and fluffy. This should take about 5 minutes.

3. With the mixer on medium (speed 4) add the eggs, one at a time, to the mixer bowl, beating well after each addition. Add in the vanilla and lemon juice. Use a spatula to scrape down the sides and bottom of the bowl to make sure everything is incorporated.

4. In a separate bowl, combine the flour, baking powder, and salt.

5. Add the dry ingredients to the wet mixture in the machine. With the mixer on low (STIR speed), mix until just combined. The batter will be a bit thicker than typical cake batter.

6. Remove the mixing bowl from the mixer and stir in 1½ cups of the blueberries by hand using a spatula. Spoon the batter into the prepared pan and spread evenly.

7. Bake until the top is golden brown and a toothpick inserted into the center of the cake comes out clean, approximately 50 minutes.

8. Transfer the pan to a cooling rack and let cool for 5 minutes. Unmold cake from the pan onto a cooling rack and cool.

9. While the cake cools, make the glaze. In a separate bowl, combine all glaze ingredients with a spoon. The consistency should be thick yet pourable. Use a toothpick to poke holes on top of cake, then pour glaze over the cooled cake. Use remaining blueberries as a garnish on top.

TRICK

If it's not blueberry season, you can use frozen blueberries. Rinse the frozen berries in a strainer under cool water until the water runs clear. Pat dry with paper towels before adding them to the cake batter.

BUTTERCAKE BAKERY CHOCOLATE CAKE

(V)

"This cake was the most popular flavor at Buttercake Bakery. It's delicious with the Buttercake Bakery Buttercream Frosting (page 195) or the Buttercake Bakery Dark Chocolate Frosting (page 196), but my family requests their birthday cakes frosted with Cream Cheese Frosting (page 207–8)." —LOGAN

1½ cups cake flour

¾ cup natural unsweetened cocoa powder (not hot chocolate mix)

1½ teaspoons baking powder

½ teaspoon salt

1 stick plus 3 tablespoons (5½ ounces) unsalted butter, room temperature

1¾ cups granulated sugar

2 large eggs, room temperature

1 teaspoon pure vanilla extract

2 cups sour cream, room temperature

1. Preheat oven to 325°F. Butter and flour cake pans, or line cupcake trays with paper liners.

2. In a small bowl, combine the cake flour, cocoa powder, baking powder, and salt and set aside.

3. In a stand mixer, cream the butter and sugar on low (speed 2) and gradually increase speed to medium (speed 4) until mixture is pale and fluffy.

4. With mixer on low (speed 2), add the eggs and vanilla and combine. Use a spatula to scrape down the sides and bottom of bowl.

TRICK

Cake flour is a finer grind than all-purpose flour; it helps make cakes light and fluffy. You can find cake flour in most supermarkets, or you can make your own. To make your own, start with 1 cup all-purpose flour. Remove 2 tablespoons of the flour and replace it by adding 2 tablespoons cornstarch. Sift all the components together and it's ready to use.

RECIPE CONTINUES ○———→

5. With the mixer on low (speed 2), alternate the dry ingredients with the sour cream (dry, wet, dry, wet, dry) in several batches. Use a spatula to scrape the sides and bottom of the bowl after each addition.

6. Divide the batter evenly between the two cake pans, or use the ice cream scoop to fill the cupcake tins.

7. Bake the cakes for 25 minutes, or 20 minutes for cupcakes, until a toothpick comes out dry.

8. Once completely cool, frost with your choice of frosting and serve. Serve warm or room temperature.

BUTTERCAKE BAKERY BUTTERCREAM FROSTING

(GF, V)

Half-and-half makes this recipe much more decadent and delicious, which is exactly what you want in a buttercream frosting.

1½ sticks (6 ounces) unsalted butter, room temperature

5 cups powdered sugar, sifted

¼ cup half-and-half

½ tablespoon pure vanilla extract

1. In the stand mixer, add all ingredients and mix on low (speed 2) and gradually increase speed to medium (speed 4) until mixture is light and fluffy.

2. Frost a thoroughly cooled cake or cupcakes.

TRICK

We love to use a mesh colander to sift ingredients. Just place the colander over a bowl and use a large serving spoon to push the powdered sugar through to remove any clumps.

BUTTERCAKE BAKERY DARK CHOCOLATE FROSTING

(GF, V)

This frosting is for the chocolate lovers. It tastes great on the Buttercake Bakery Chocolate Cake (page 192–94) or just on a spoon.

6 ounces unsweetened chocolate

2 sticks (8 ounces) unsalted butter, room temperature

2 cups powdered sugar, sifted

1 tablespoon pure vanilla extract

pinch of salt

1. Over medium heat, set up a double boiler by placing a metal or glass mixing bowl over a small pot of simmering water. Place the unsweetened chocolate in the bowl over the simmering water until it all melts and becomes smooth. Remove from heat, set aside and let cool for 10 minutes.

2. In the bowl of the stand mixer, cream the butter and powdered sugar on low (speed 2) and gradually increase speed to medium (speed 4) until mixture is pale and fluffy.

3. Add in the cooled chocolate, vanilla and salt. Beat on medium speed (speed 4) until shiny and smooth. Scrape down the sides with a spatula.

4. Frost a completely cooled cake or cupcakes.

LINDA'S CHOCOLATE CHIP COOKIE PIE

(V)

This recipe was contributed by guest chef Ricky Strauss.

"When I was going to sleepaway camp in the summer (Camp Kennybrook, NY), my mother used to make this for me on parent's visiting day. I would always be the most popular kid in my bunk, because everyone flipped for this dessert! Even today, it still reminds me of home and my mom's terrific cooking. I've found it's the perfect go-to dessert for a crowd!" —RICKY

CRUST

1½ cups graham cracker crumbs

⅓ cup granulated sugar

6 tablespoons unsalted butter, melted

FILLING

1 stick (4 ounces) unsalted butter, room temperature

1 cup granulated sugar

2 large eggs, room temperature

½ cup all-purpose flour

1 cup semi-sweet chocolate chips

1. If making your own crust, preheat oven to 325°F. If using a premade crust, skip to step 4.

2. To make the crust, use a metal fork to mix the graham cracker crumbs, sugar, and melted butter together in a small bowl. Once combined, use your hands or a spoon to spread the mixture into the bottom and sides of an 8-inch pie pan. The crust should reach about halfway up the sides.

3. Bake for 7 minutes at 325°F. Remove and let cool for 15 minutes while preparing the filling.

TRICK

If you're short on time, there are premade graham cracker crusts that are very good and nobody will know you cheated. If using a pre-made piecrust, no need to bake it ahead of time, skip to step 4.

RECIPE CONTINUES ○——→

4. Raise oven temperature to 350°F.

5. In a stand mixer, cream the butter and sugar starting on low (speed 2) and increasing to medium (speed 4) until light and fluffy. Add eggs, one at a time, combining well after each addition.

6. With the mixer on low (speed 2) add the flour until just combined.

7. Remove bowl from stand mixer and stir in the chocolate chips with a spatula to disperse the chips evenly throughout the batter.

8. Pour batter into the crust and bake at 350°F for 40 minutes or until center is set and the top is golden brown.

9. Let cool slightly, cut into 8 wedges, and serve with vanilla ice cream.

BUTTERCAKE BAKERY PECAN SNOWBALLS

(V)

Did you know that the pecan is technically not a nut? For reals. It's actually called a "drupe," which is a fruit with a single stone or pit surrounded by a husk, like a peach or a plum. Tons of drupes have been masquerading as nuts for years, the walnut and almond included. You can't say you don't learn something new with each recipe here at *The Kitchen Decoded*. These pecan-filled powdered-sugar-covered snowball cookies are so sweet and crunchy, you'll want to pop the entire dozen in your mouth one right after the other. They're a holiday favorite but we enjoy them all year long.

2 sticks (8 ounces) unsalted butter, room temperature

½ cup + 1 cup powdered sugar, divided

1 teaspoon pure vanilla extract

2¼ cups all-purpose flour

¼ teaspoon salt

¾ cup chopped pecans

1. Preheat oven to 350°F. Place parchment paper (or silicone baking mat) on the cookie sheet.

2. In a stand mixer fitted with the flat beater, combine the butter, ½ cup powdered sugar, and vanilla on low (speed 2), gradually increasing speed to medium (speed 4) until mixture is pale and fluffy.

3. When well combined, on low (speed 2) add the flour and salt, then pecans. Use a spatula to scrape the sides and bottom of the pan to make sure all the ingredients are mixed together.

4. Use an ice cream scoop to drop balls of batter onto a lined baking sheet. Bake 10–12 minutes, until tops are golden brown.

RECIPE CONTINUES ○——→

5. Remove cookies from oven and let them cool slightly, about 3 minutes.

6. While the cookies are still warm, place sugar in a sieve and sprinkle over the cookies. Place the cookies on a cooling rack set inside a baking sheet to catch the sugar that may fall off. Then refill the sieve with powdered sugar and sprinkle the cookies a second time to get them extra coated.

TRICK

Kick up the holiday cheer and coat the cookies with candy cane dust. Add 1 teaspoon peppermint extract when you add the vanilla. To make the coating, place 12 small candy canes in a food processor with the chopping blade. Turn on and let run for about 45 seconds until the candy canes turn into a fine pink dust. Place crushed candy canes in a bowl with a ¼ cup powdered sugar. While the cookies are still warm, roll them in the candy cane mixture.

CITRUS ALMOND CAKE

(GF, V)

If you're in search of a great dessert for guests with wheat allergies, rejoice! This cake is light, fluffy, delicious, and entirely gluten-free. The base is made from ground almonds, which are packed with healthy vitamins like potassium, vitamin E, and magnesium. It's the perfect dessert to serve after a heavy meal.

4 eggs, yolks and whites separated, room temperature

zest from 1 lemon

zest from 1 orange plus 1 tablespoon orange juice

¼ teaspoon pure vanilla extract

½ cup granulated sugar, divided in half

1½ cups finely ground almond flour (also called almond meal)

¼ teaspoon ground cinnamon

1 teaspoon baking powder

pinch of salt

1 teaspoon white vinegar

2 tablespoons powdered sugar for sprinkling on top of baked cake

TRICK

If almond flour is not available at your market, you can make it with your food processor. Place 1 ½ cups blanched, slivered almonds in your food processor with the chopping blade and pulse until finely ground.

1. Preheat oven to 350°F. Place a round of parchment paper on the bottom of a 9-inch springform pan, and grease it and the sides of the pan with butter or nonstick cooking spray.

2. In a large mixing bowl, mix the egg yolks, lemon and orange zests, orange juice, vanilla, and ¼ cup sugar with a wooden spoon until smooth.

3. In a separate bowl, combine the almond flour, cinnamon, and baking powder. Add the almond mixture to the egg yolk mixture and stir with a spoon until well combined.

4. In a stand mixer with the wire whip/whisk attachment, beat the egg whites, starting on low (speed 2) and gradually increasing the speed to high (speed 6). When bubbles start to form, add a pinch of salt and the vinegar. After 3 minutes of beating, slowly add the remaining ¼ cup sugar. Continue beating for 2 more minutes, until soft peaks form (soft peaks = tips of peaks fall over when wire whip/whisk is removed).

RECIPE CONTINUES ○——————→

5. Add the egg whites into the almond mixture in small batches. Use a spatula to gently fold a scoop of egg whites over on top of itself a few times. In order to keep the whipped eggs intact, you don't want to stir with too much force. It will seem a bit goopy and the egg whites won't seamlessly incorporate into the almond mixture at first. After you add 2–3 additions of egg whites, the batter will start to get fluffy and smoother. Keep using a folding technique so as not to deflate the egg whites.

6. Pour batter into the prepared pan and place in the oven. Bake for 25–30 minutes or until top is golden brown. Remove from the oven and let cool. Run a sharp knife around the edge to help release the sides, and gently remove the cake to a serving plate. Place powdered sugar in a mesh sieve and sprinkle over the cake before serving.

BUTTERCAKE BAKERY PUMPKIN WHOOPIE PIES

(V)

Ever wonder where the whoopie pie got its name? Legend has it that Amish women hid these cakey, cream-filled sandwich cookies in their husband's lunch pails and when the farmers found them, they shouted, "Whoopie!" Get ready to elicit the same reaction from guests when they take a bite of these Buttercake Bakery Pumpkin Whoopie Pies filled with delectable Cream Cheese Frosting. "Customers at Buttercake Bakery couldn't wait for October 1, when we would makes these for the first time each year." —LOGAN

WHOOPIE PIES

3 cups all-purpose flour

1 teaspoon salt

1 teaspoon baking powder

1 teaspoon baking soda

2 tablespoons ground cinnamon

1 tablespoon ground ginger

1 tablespoon ground cloves

2 cups packed brown sugar

2 sticks (8 ounces) unsalted butter, room temperature

2 eggs, room temperature

1 teaspoon pure vanilla extract

3 cups canned pumpkin puree

CREAM CHEESE FROSTING

1 stick (4 ounces) unsalted butter, room temperature

I package (8 ounces) cream cheese, room temperature

3 cups powdered sugar, sifted

1 teaspoon pure vanilla extract

RECIPE CONTINUES ⚬———→

1. Preheat oven to 350°F. Line two cookie sheets with parchment paper.

2. In a large bowl, combine the flour, salt, baking powder, baking soda, cinnamon, ginger, and cloves and set aside.

3. In a stand mixer on low (speed 2), cream the brown sugar and butter, gradually increasing speed to medium (speed 4) until light and fluffy. Add the eggs and vanilla on low (speed 2) until combined. Use a spatula to scrape down the sides and bottom of the bowl.

4. With the mixer on low (speed 2), alternate the dry ingredients with the pumpkin (dry, wet, dry, wet, dry) in several batches. Scrape the sides of the mixer with a spatula after each addition to make sure all ingredients are incorporated.

5. Use the medium ice cream scoop to drop batter onto the parchment-lined cookie sheets 1 inch apart.

6. Bake for 12 minutes, turning the pans 180 degrees once about halfway through baking.

7. Remove the cookies from the oven and let cool completely on a cooling rack.

8. While the cookies cool, combine all the frosting ingredients in the stand mixer on low (speed 2) until light and fluffy.

9. Once cookies are completely cool, use a small ice cream scoop or spoon and cover half of the cookies with a small scoop of icing. Place the other half of the cookies on top to create a sandwich.

TRICK

The batter can also be used to make pumpkin bread. Divide the cookie batter between 2 buttered and floured 9 x 5 x 4-inch loaf pans and bake at 350°F for 40-50 minutes.

BUTTERCAKE BAKERY CHEESECAKE

(V)

The advent of this dessert dates all the way back to ancient Greece when a physician named Aegimius wrote a book on the art of making cheesecake. You know what that means? A doctor wrote the book on cheesecake, so it must be good for you. Right? We like to think so. Creamy, rich, and sweet, this cheesecake is destined to impress.

CRUST

1¼ cups graham cracker crumbs

¼ cup granulated sugar

⅓ cup unsalted butter, melted

CHEESECAKE BATTER

4 packages (2 pounds) cream cheese, room temperature

1¾ cups granulated sugar

2 tablespoons lemon juice

2 teaspoons pure vanilla extract

4 eggs, room temperature

1. Preheat oven to 325°F.

2. Butter a 9-inch springform pan. Tightly wrap the outside of the pan with tin foil to prevent water from seeping in during the cooking process.

3. Mix all ingredients for the crust in a small bowl to incorporate. Then press it into the bottom of the buttered springform pan and bake for 15 minutes.

4. While the crust bakes, make the filling. In a stand mixer, beat the cream cheese on medium (speed 4) until absolutely smooth.

5. With the mixer on medium (speed 4) add the sugar, lemon juice, and vanilla. Beat until well combined. Use a spatula to scrape batter from the sides and bottom of the bowl to make sure everything is well incorporated.

RECIPE CONTINUES ⟶

6. Add the eggs to the batter, one at a time, mixing on medium (speed 4.) Use a spatula to scrape down the sides of the bowl after each addition.

7. Pour the batter into the springform pan over the top of the baked crust. Tap the bottom of the pan on the table to get out any air bubbles.

8. Place the springform into the larger pan (9 x 13-inch) and fill it with 1½ inches water to create a water bath. This will help the cheesecake bake evenly.

9. Place the pans in the oven and bake for 60 minutes, until the cheesecake is set but still jiggles. Try not to open the oven more than once during baking, as this can create cracks on the top of the cake. After 60 minutes, turn OFF the oven but leave the cheesecake inside for an additional hour, allowing the cheesecake to cool slowly. Remove the cheesecake from the oven, take off the foil, and refrigerate overnight. When ready to serve, remove from springform pan.

TRICK

Baking the cheesecake in a water bath helps the cake cook evenly, and cooling it in a warm oven prevents the surface from cracking.

BROWN SUGAR MERINGUE BERRY STACK

(GF, V)

"I'm not a chocolate person, but anything with whipped cream and berries is my mainstay. Enter these delicious Brown Sugar Meringue Berry Stacks. They're light, gluten-free, and refreshing." —LOGAN

MERINGUE

½ cup granulated sugar

¼ cup packed brown sugar

¾ teaspoon cornstarch

3 egg whites, room temperature

pinch of salt

1 teaspoon distilled white vinegar

¾ teaspoon pure vanilla extract

BERRIES

3 pints mixed berries (cut in half if large)

2 tablespoons granulated sugar

WHIPPED CREAM

1 cup heavy cream, chilled

1 tablespoon granulated sugar

½ teaspoon pure vanilla extract

1. Preheat oven to 275°F. Place a sheet of parchment paper on a cookie sheet.

2. In a small bowl, combine sugar, brown sugar, and cornstarch, and set aside.

3. In a stand mixer fitted with the wire whip/whisk attachment, add the egg whites and a pinch of salt and beat on medium (speed 4) for 3 minutes until soft peaks form (soft peaks = tips of peaks fall over when wire whip is removed).

4. With stand mixer set to medium (speed 4), add the sugar mixture 1 tablespoon at a time. Once all the sugar has been mixed in, add in the vinegar and vanilla, then turn up the speed to high (speed 6) and beat for 5 minutes until the meringue is glossy.

TRICK

Any trace of grease will ruin your meringue, so make sure your spatula, mixing bowl, and whisk attachment are very clean. To make sure, wipe them down with a paper towel moistened with vinegar. You can also make the meringue the day before and cover it with tin foil. Place it in back the oven at 200°F for 2 minutes to crisp it back up before using.

RECIPE CONTINUES ○⟶

5. On the prepared cookie sheet, use a spatula to spread the meringue so it's about a ½-inch thick. Leave at least a 1-inch border of space all the way around the pan so that you can easily remove the hardened meringue later. Bake for 30–35 minutes.

6. Once cooked, leave meringue in the oven but turn the oven OFF. Let the meringue cool inside the warm oven for 30 minutes. Then remove pan from the oven and allow to cool completely.

7. While meringue cools, mix the berries and sugar in a medium mixing bowl and let stand at room temperature for an hour.

8. For the whipped cream, add all ingredients into the stand mixer with the wire whip/whisk attachment and mix on high (speed 6) for 5 minutes until soft peaks form.

9. Once meringue has cooled, break it up into chunks. Create the stacks by layering meringue pieces, berries, and cream in glasses or jars.

ROSEMARY SEA SALT FOCACCIA

(DF, V)

Focaccia, while tantalizing on the taste buds, usually takes way too long to bake . . . until now! We've got a little trick that will have homemade focaccia coming out of your oven in under an hour. Doughy and salty with hints of rosemary, it's about as close as you can get to Italy without leaving your house.

1 packet (¼ ounce) active dry yeast

1 teaspoon granulated sugar

1 cup warm water (about 100°F)

3 cups all-purpose flour

2 teaspoons salt, plus extra for sprinkling (if you have sea salt flakes, use them for sprinkling)

1 teaspoon dried rosemary

3 tablespoons extra-virgin olive oil, plus extra for greasing pans

TRICK

The proofing process (allowing the dough to rise) is sped up by putting the dough in a warm oven for twenty minutes. This dough also makes a great homemade pizza dough. Just remove the rosemary and add sauce and cheese and bake.

1. Preheat oven to 200°F. Oil baking pan (pour a little olive oil into the pan and swish it around to coat the bottom and sides).

2. In a clear measuring cup, combine yeast, sugar, and water. Make sure the yeast bubbles produce approximately ¼ cup foam. This should take 5 minutes. If foam does not appear, start this step over.

3. In a stand mixer with the dough hook, add flour, salt, rosemary, and olive oil. Turn mixer to low (speed 2) and slowly add water and yeast mixture. Mix on medium (speed 4) until the dough pulls away from the sides, about 5 minutes, but is still sticky.

4. Shape the dough into a ball and place it in the oiled pan. Put the pan in the oven at 200°F for 20 minutes.

5. Remove the dough from the oven. It will have grown in size. Flip the dough over so both sides are well oiled. (Be careful, the pan and dough will be hot!) Stretch the dough to fit the pan. Use your fingers to create indentations in the dough; this will give it that signature focaccia uneven texture. Sprinkle the top with extra salt flakes and drizzle with extra-virgin olive oil.

6. Raise the oven temperature to 400°F.

7. Place pan back in the oven and bake at 400°F for 20 minutes. Serve warm or at room temperature.

CHAPTER 7

LET'S GET THIS PARTY PLANNED!

IN THIS CHAPTER

RULES FOR HOSTING   221

GENERAL TIPS AND TRICKS FOR HOSTING   222

MENU PLANNING   227

Break out the party hats and champagne! It's time to celebrate. Now that we've armed you with foolproof recipes and given you the lowdown on all the best kitchen tools and tricks, invite a few friends over and practice your newfound skills. In this chapter you'll find rules, checklists, and sample menus to effortlessly entertain guests in your home.

RULES FOR HOSTING

RULE #1: GET ORGANIZED FOR PARTIES BIG AND SMALL

Not every get-together has to be a big production or sit-down dinner, but being organized helps streamline preparation. Plan the menu well in advance of your event. Write down ingredients for a shopping list and go to a market that carries most, if not all, of your items. Having to shop at four different locations is exhausting, and you need all your energy to get the party started. Make a guest list and send out invitations three to four weeks before the party. Confirm attendance and keep a tally of how many people have RSVP'd. Take an inventory of serving platters and utensils. Use sticky notes to indicate which platter will be used for each dish to ensure that you have enough to cover the entire meal. Recruit a friend to be your helper. Having an extra set of hands for prep work or cleanup is invaluable. Plus, friends = fun.

RULE #2: REMEMBER TO HAVE FUN!

We've said it before and we'll say it again. Fun is the key to cooking and successfully hosting guests in your home. Finally make use of that good china and crystal you've been storing in the garage, or keep it casual with festive paper goods to save time on cleanup. Either way, you can create a party atmosphere for a memorable occasion. Small touches like votive candles, an inspired soundtrack, party favors, and flowers create a mood that tells your guests, "I'm really happy you are here!" That message will rub off on every person who walks through the door, and a good time will be had by all. Whether you're entertaining one guest or twenty, greet each person when they show up, and take the time to celebrate all the hard work that went into preparing for the event. That means join the party! Walk around and try to talk to everyone, even if it's just to dole out hugs or quickly catch up. Don't spend all night in the kitchen cooking and cleaning, because that is absolutely no fun.

GENERAL TIPS AND TRICKS FOR HOSTING

INVITING GUESTS

- Establish the time and date for your event first and work backwards to get everything done in time.
- Let guests know the dress code, i.e., casual, cocktail attire, dressy, black and white, hats and wigs, anything goes! As the host, get dolled up. Ditch the sweatpants and let your guests know that spending time with them is a special occasion.
- Invite people who enjoy socializing. Separate couples.
- Encourage your guests to meet someone new by assigning spots at the table with seating cards. Write names on both sides of the seating card so people across the table can read it.
- Introduce guests to each other with a little anecdote about how you met.

WHAT'S ON THE MENU?

- Be sure to ask your guests if they have any food restrictions or allergies before you plan the menu. If you're setting up food buffet style, label the dishes. Everyone likes to know what he or she is eating.
- Use seasonal ingredients that are less expensive and more delicious.
- Prepare the last course first and get it out of the way. Most desserts can be made ahead of time, like our Classic Chocolate Pudding (pages 137–138), Panna Cotta (page 140), Citrus Almond Cake (pages 204–206), and Linda's Chocolate Chip Cookie Pie (pages 198–200).
- Choose a course with flavors that will enhance overnight. Our suggestions include: Roasted Tomato Soup (page 98), Wine-Braised Brisket (page 166), or Vegetable Coconut Curry (page 162). The day of the get-together, you want to limit yourself to assembling and warming up dishes. Most of your work should be done by the time the guests arrive.
- Serve comfort food. When entertaining, it's never a good time to test a new recipe. Go with something tried and true.
- Easy appetizers, cheese platters, and light snacks are perfect for casual get-togethers like book club meetings or board game night. No need to prepare a huge feast.
- For cocktail parties, count on having ten appetizers per person and six per person for dinner parties. It's wise to err on the side of having too much food so nobody will go hungry.
- Try placing dishes right on the table and let people pass them around family style. This casual atmosphere encourages guests to chat.

RAISE A GLASS

- When it comes to wine, sauvignon blanc and cabernet sauvignon are good choices. Most people like them and they taste great with almost every dish. Sparkling wine like prosecco or cava gives a celebratory air. Have a bottle or two at the ready for toasts. If you're not sure which label to buy, ask the wine expert at the store and give them a budget to work within. They can help you figure out which wine will taste best with your menu at the right price.

- Create a signature or themed cocktail like our Velvet Hammer Sangria (page 142) or Raspberry Jalapeño Limeade (page 86) and you won't need to buy a ton of different cocktail fixings—just make a big batch in advance. No need to run around mixing drinks on the fly. You should have enough ingredients for one drink per hour per guest. Don't forget non-alcoholic options.

- Spread drink and appetizer stations around the room to encourage party flow.

- For large parties with more than twenty-five guests, consider hiring a bartender who can also help clean up. A good bartender keeps the drinks flowing, and you get to mingle with guests. Someone to keep the kitchen tidy during and after the party will spare you from facing a giant mess after the guests depart. Contact staffing agencies or ask friends for recommendations.

- If a bartender isn't in the budget, let the guests play bartender. Set up a self-serve bar area with a few cocktail recipes tacked up on the wall and all the required ingredients. It's another fun way to get folks socializing.

- Have lots and lots of ice on hand. If you can't cram enough bags into the freezer, fill an ice chest and keep it near the bar area.

CROSS TASKS OFF OF THE LIST AHEAD OF TIME

- Set the table the night before and it's one less thing on your to-do list the day of the soirée. When setting the table, make sure the knife blade faces in towards the plate.

- Freeze candlesticks one to two days prior to the event to prevent wax from dripping on the table the night of the party.

- Clear out room in the closet and have extra hangers on hand for guests to hang their coats. Or if you're going to allow friends to stow coats and handbags in a bedroom, make sure to neaten up first.

- Create a mood. Pick up some unscented votive candles and place them in the center of the table. Get bunches of big blooms like hydrangeas, peonies, or dahlias to brighten up the table and serving areas. You won't have to purchase as many flowers if you choose larger blooms. Keep the centerpieces low enough that guests can see each other across the table. A bowl or platter of fruit is also an attractive centerpiece for casual get-togethers.

- If you have a friend or two helping in the kitchen, set aside snacks and drinks to keep them fueled and happy.
- Transfer condiments like ketchup, mustard, soy sauce, salt, and pepper into glass bowls, a muffin tin, ramekins, teacups, or jars. Be creative! It's a simple added touch that makes your table look inviting.
- Don't run out of toilet paper or other essentials. Stock the restroom with enough hand towels and toilet paper to accommodate more than the number of guests invited.
- Hosting an outdoor event? Get citronella candles to keep the bugs off the guests and the food.

RAISE THE ROOF—PREPARING FOR LARGE GET-TOGETHERS

- Do you have enough room for everyone at your dining table? You can always borrow a few things from friends, but for big quantities, rent extra chairs, tables, serving dishes, and flatware from party supply companies. It's surprisingly reasonable, and they will deliver and pick up. You do need to reserve everything at least two weeks in advance, especially during a holiday season.
- When a lot of people get together, things get knocked over. Stash your delicate, valuable, and easily breakable possessions in a bedroom. And if something does break, just let it go and say, "I always hated that thing!"
- Buy the appetizers. No need to be a superhero. Pick up premade dips, veggie platters, olives, nuts, and cheeses at the store and transfer them onto cute serving dishes. Spread them around the party for people to snack on.
- If your fridge is too packed for your large dinner, use an ice chest with ice to store meat and perishables inside.

HAPPY HOLIDAY HOSTING TIPS

- Consider inviting friends over who live far away from their families at holiday time. Be open to guests bringing another "orphan" to your party. The more the merrier!
- Create centerpieces by filling a glass bowl full of multicolored glass ball ornaments for a cheerful pop of color.
- An inexpensive way to create mood lighting is to switch out white bulbs for colored bulbs that match the theme or spirit of the party.
- Fill the house with a wonderful holiday aroma: Boil a pot of water with orange rind, cinnamon sticks, whole star anise, and whole cloves.
- Put together a fun holiday playlist or stream one through Pandora, Spotify, or iTunes Radio. Or assign a couple of friends to play DJ and ask them to

bring playlists on their phones that can be hooked up to a docking station. Music should be loud enough that people can hear what's playing but not so loud that they have to shout at each other.

- White elephant gift exchanges are another great way to encourage guests to interact. Ask friends to bring a generic wrapped gift costing $10–$20. Each guest is assigned a number and when the number is called, they can choose a gift, or take one that has already been opened. If they "steal" the gift from someone, that person gets to choose a new unopened gift. A gift can only be stolen three times, which helps move the game along.

KEEP IT LIGHT AND MERRY

- Get the guests mingling with a fun party game. Write a bunch of celebrity names on nametags. When friends arrive, you or your assigned party helper will place the nametag on the guest's back so they can't see it. They will need to walk around and ask other party attendees to give them hints about the identity of their hidden celebrity name.
- If you have pets that enjoy big get-togethers, dress them up for the occasion by placing a bow on their collars and let them be part of the festivities. For outdoor parties, let friends bring their well-behaved pets along. But if your pets get nervous around a lot of noise, put them in a quiet room away from the chaos.

- Take pictures or delegate a friend to capture the memories with a camera or phone. Send photo highlights out the next day or create a gallery online.

OPERATION CLEAN UP

- Empty the dishwasher before guests arrive. Fill a bucket or plastic bin with soapy water, and when plates come back from the dinner table, toss them in the bucket to soak. That makes the end-of-the-night job a whole lot easier and keeps your sink from overflowing.
- Clean as you go. Tidy up after cooking each course to keep your kitchen looking party ready.
- If you have the budget, hire someone to help clean up. Cooking, hosting, and mingling is a full-time job on the big day. The last thing you want to deal with once everyone leaves is a huge pile of dishes. Hire someone through a staffing agency, or ask friends if they know any great taskmasters or professional cleaners.

AU REVOIR, ADIOS, AUF WIEDERSEHEN, AND GOODBYE

- Some people have so much fun at parties, they never want to leave. But hosting is exhausting and chances are, you'll be ready to collapse onto a pile of soft pillows long before the conga line disbands. To wind things down, brew a big pot of coffee and tea and get ready to send people on their way home.

- Pick up white Chinese food takeout boxes to fill with leftovers, and send guests home with a few. Cheap deli containers will work too, so you don't have to give away your good containers.
- Parting gifts also help scoot people out the door at the end of the night. Here are some ideas:
  - **Pumpkin Pie Spice in small jars:** To make 8 tablespoons Pumpkin Pie Spice, combine 4 tablespoons ground cinnamon, 4 teaspoons ground ginger, 4 teaspoons nutmeg, 3 teaspoons ground allspice, and 3 teaspoons ground cloves. Put the spice in little glass jars for guests to take home.
  - **Holiday potpourri pack:** In cellophane, bag up dried orange rind, cloves, star anise and cinnamon sticks. Tie it with a bow and give it to guests as a parting gift.
  - **Dry or Jerk Spice Rub (page 16):** Bag it or jar it as a parting gift for guests.
  - **Kettle Corn (page 170) or Mom's Chocolate Chip Toffee Cookies (page 38):** These addictive treats look cute in cellophane bags wrapped up with a bow.

GOOD MANNERS

- If guests brought gifts, flowers, food, or wine to the party, send a handwritten thank you note the next day. And don't forget a special gift and note for the party helpers.
- Downplay mistakes: to err is human; to quickly move on is divine. :)

MENU PLANNING

We've compiled several tasty recipes into sample menus for your upcoming events. But don't feel pressured to make a three-course meal all on your own. Ask friends to bring drinks or dessert to cut a few corners. You do not have to make everything from scratch! Pick up items like fresh fruit, dinner rolls, bags of salad greens, dips, cheeses, ice cream, and premade side dishes from the grocery store, specialty market, or local farmers market.

BRUNCH

Buttercake Bakery Orange Currant Scones (pages 120–21)

Sundried Tomato Basil Frittatas (page 28)

Granola (page 94)

SPECIAL OCCASION LUNCH

Feta Dip (page 122)

Quinoa Tabbouleh (pages 66–67)

Tandoori Salmon Salad (page 130)

Buttercake Bakery Pecan Snowballs (pages 201–2)

ITALIAN SUNDAY SUPPER

Arugula Salad with Lemon Vinaigrette (page 27)

Spaghetti and Turkey Meatballs (page 32) with Aunt Andrea's Red Sauce (page 34)

Panna Cotta (page 140)

WEEK NIGHT DINNER FOR TWO

Arugula Salad with Lemon Vinaigrette (page 27)

Halibut with Couscous and Sundried Tomatoes (page 168)

Apple Blackberry Cobbler (page 84)

BETTER THAN TAKE-OUT

Cold Asian Peanut Noodle Salad (page 128)

Coleslaw with Sesame Dressing (page 25)

Pork Loin with Asian Marinade (page 21)

MEATLESS MONDAY OR VEGETARIAN OPTION

Option 1:

Salad with Basil Balsamic Dressing (page 25)

Vegetable Coconut Curry with Rice (page 162)

Buttercake Bakery Banana Cake (pages 187–88)

Option 2:

Black Bean Patties (page 78)

Baked Sweet Potato Fries (page 106)

Cora's Sliced Sweet Pickles (page 150)

Donut Holes (page 172)

BIRTHDAY

Caesar Salad with Eggless Caesar Dressing (page 26)

Cheese Drawer Mac and Cheese (pages 81–82)

Buttercake Bakery Chocolate Cake (pages 192–94)

GAME DAY/SUPER BOWL

Guacamole (page 56), Roasted Salsa (page 59), Melissa's Bean Dip (page 58)

Oven-Baked Chicken Wings (page 112)

Turkey Chili (pages 160–61)

Buttercake Bakery Brownies (page 40)

BACKYARD BBQ

Grilled Asparagus with Truffle Oil (page 124)

Backyard Citrus Chicken (page 132)

Velvet Hammer Sangria (page 142)

Brown Sugar Meringue Berry Stacks (pages 213–14)

INDOOR BBQ

Cornbread Panzanella (page 100)

Indoor Dry Rub Ribs (page 110)

Mom's Chocolate Chip Toffee Cookies (page 38)

BAKE SALE

Buttercake Bakery Lemon Bars (pages 134–36)

Buttercake Bakery Chocolate Cake/Cupcakes (pages 192–94)

Kettle Corn (page 170)

EASY DINNER PARTY

Option 1:

Salad with Basil Balsamic Dressing (page 25)

Mussels with Sausage (page 158)

Citrus Almond Cake (pages 204–6)

Option 2:

Mediterranean Beef Stew (page 156)

Scallion Parmesan Drop Biscuits (page 70)

Linda's Chocolate Chip Cookie Pie (pages 198–200)

HOLIDAYS

Option 1:

Creamed Spinach (page 126)

Mashed Potatoes (page 30)

Whole Roasted Chicken (page 36)

Buttercake Bakery Pumpkin Whoopie Pies (pages 207–8)

Option 2:

Lemon Dijon Roasted Brussels Sprouts (page 104)

Wine-Braised Brisket (page 166)

Buttercake Bakery Pecan Snowballs (pages 201–2)

ACKNOWLEDGMENTS

We have massive amounts of gratitude for all the family, friends, and companies who helped us on this journey with love, support, recipes, testing, and product contribution.

Logan's Family & Friends

Alison and Brian Levant, Taylor Levant, Aaron and Laura Levant, Renee Logan, Carole Pohn, Liz Laffont, Melissa and Matt Ehlke, Rudy Dobrev, Tony Lipp, Claire Zimmerman, Erica Domesek and Kristi Reilly

Hilary's Family & Friends

Jared Mazzaschi, Chris Hattenbach, Judith Eytel, Edward Swar, Mary Kula, Tracy Sunrize Johnson, Martine Trélaün, Jason White, Elizabeth Ross, Josh Hauke, Cindy Lin, Lilliam Rivera, Mary Shannon, Frances Sackett, Shea Cunningham, Ted Swiet, Jessie Rogers, Lynn Hirshfield, Kevin Campbell, Jessica Intihar, Stephanie Kluft, Theresa Cross, Jan Coleman, Sandra Nieto

Guest Chefs

Melissa Ehlke, Liz Laffont, Alison Levant, Tony Lipp, Kristin Stark, and Ricky Strauss

Big round of applause to all the tireless testers who shopped, cooked, and provided detailed notes for each recipe. We heart you: Samantha and Jason Goldstein, Blake and Lisa Pick, Casey Morris, Marni Richman, Shadi Mullin, Shauna Sever, Robyn and Nick Aguirre, Marie Therese Aguirre, Carolyn Averill, Susan Grover, Jaime Jones, Kimmy Kertes, Lucy Bennett, Deanna Clower, Hardeep Birdi, Patti Kudish, Lesley and Michael LeFetra, Diane Dufau, Amy Cohen, Alex Zornizer, Susan Chen, Gillian Brecker, Michelle Cox, Jason Klein, Wendy Blasdel, Allyson Whitfield, and Jessie Nagel.

Tip of the hat to *Alton Brown's Gear for Your Kitchen* and Bee Wilson's *Consider the Fork*, both excellent references for cooking and equipment history.

Virtual high fives to all the manufacturers who gave us permission to use their products and contributed tools for our photo shoot.
Cuisinart: Dan Kulp
Microplane: Julia Stambules and Gracie Rizzo
Le Creuset: Claire Femiani
OXO: Emily Forrest and Monica Chen

Extra special thanks to the lovely ladies who helped bring the idea of THE KITCHEN DECODED to life and made our book beautiful.
Food Photographer: Melissa Barnes
Food and Prop Stylist: Alicia Buszczak
Photo Shoot Assistant: Octavia Klein
Book Designer: Tracy Sunrize Johnson
Book Editor: Lindsey Breuer

METRIC CONVERSIONS

Metric and Imperial Conversions
(These conversions are rounded for convenience)

Ingredient	Cups/Tablespoons/Teaspoons	Ounces	Grams/Milliliters
Butter	1 cup=16 tablespoons= 2 sticks	8 ounces	230 grams
Cream cheese	1 tablespoon	0.5 ounce	14.5 grams
Cheese, shredded	1 cup	4 ounces	110 grams
Cornstarch	1 tablespoon	0.3 ounce	8 grams
Flour, all-purpose	1 cup/1 tablespoon	4.5 ounces/ 0.3 ounce	125 grams/ 8 grams
Flour, whole wheat	1 cup	4 ounces	120 grams
Fruit, dried	1 cup	4 ounces	120 grams
Fruits or veggies, chopped	1 cup	5 to 7 ounces	145 to 200 grams
Fruits or veggies, puréed	1 cup	8.5 ounces	245 grams
Honey, maple syrup, or corn syrup	1 tablespoon	.75 ounce	20 grams
Liquids: cream, milk, water, or juice	1 cup	8 fluid ounces	240 milliliters
Oats	1 cup	5.5 ounces	150 grams
Salt	1 teaspoon	0.2 ounces	6 grams
Spices: cinnamon, cloves, ginger, or nutmeg (ground)	1 teaspoon	0.2 ounce	5 milliliters
Sugar, brown, firmly packed	1 cup	7 ounces	200 grams
Sugar, white	1 cup/1 tablespoon	7 ounces/ 0.5 ounce	200 grams/ 12.5 grams
Vanilla extract	1 teaspoon	0.2 ounce	4 grams

Oven Temperatures

Fahrenheit	Celsius	Gas Mark
225°	110°	$\frac{1}{4}$
250°	120°	$\frac{1}{2}$
275°	140°	1
300°	150°	2
325°	160°	3
350°	180°	4
375°	190°	5
400°	200°	6
425°	220°	7
450°	230°	8

INDEX

Apple Blackberry Cobbler, 84

Arugula Pesto, 62

Asian Marinade, 21

Aunt Andrea's Red Sauce, 34

Backyard Citrus Chicken, 132

Baked Brie, Three-Pepper Jelly and, 68

Baked Sweet Potato Fries, 106

Banana Cake, Buttercake Bakery,
	187–88

Basil
	Basil Balsamic Dressing, 25
	Soy Balsamic Marinade, 21
	Sundried Tomato Basil Frittatas, 28

BBQ Sauce, 18

Berry Butter, 74

Black Bean Patties, 78

Blueberry Cake, Buttercake Bakery,
	190–91

Blue Cheese Sundried Tomato Butter,
	74

Blue Cheese Vinaigrette, 27

Brisket, Wine-Braised, 166

Brownies, Buttercake Bakery, 40

Brown Sugar Butter, 74

Brown Sugar Meringue Berry Stack,
	213–14

Bruschetta, 60

Buttercake Bakery Recipes
	Banana Cake, 187–88
	Blueberry Cake, 190–91
	Brownies, 40

Buttercream Frosting, 195

Cheesecake, 210–12

Chocolate Cake, 192–94

Coffee Cake, 184–86

Dark Chocolate Frosting, 196

Lemon Bars, 134–36

Orange Currant Scones, 120–21

Pecan Snowball Cookies, 201–2

Pumpkin Whoopie Pies, 207–8

Buttercream Frosting, Buttercake
	Bakery, 195

Cheesecake, Buttercake Bakery, 210–12

Cheese Drawer Mac and Cheese, 81–82

Chicken
	Backyard Citrus Chicken, 132
	Chicken and Chorizo Paella, 164–65
	Chicken Stock, 35
	Oven-Baked Chicken Wings, 112
	Whole Roasted Chicken, 36

Chimichurri Sauce, 20

Chocolate
	Buttercake Bakery Brownies, 40
	Buttercake Bakery Chocolate Cake,
		192–94
	Buttercake Bakery Dark Chocolate
		Frosting, 196
	Classic Chocolate Pudding, 137–38
	Linda's Chocolate Chip Cookie Pie,
		198–200
	Mom's Chocolate Chip Toffee
		Cookies, 38

Citrus Almond Cake, 204–6

Classic Chocolate Pudding, 137–38

Coconut
	Coconut Rice, 152
	Vegetable Coconut Curry, 162

Coffee Cake, Buttercake Bakery,
	184–86

Cold Asian Peanut Noodle Salad, 128

Compound Butters
	Berry Butter, 74
	Blue Cheese Sundried Tomato
		Butter, 74
	Brown Sugar Butter, 74
	Herb Butter, 72
	Sriracha-Honey Butter, 74

Cora's Sliced Sweet Pickles, 150

Cornbread Panzanella, 100

Cream Cheese Frosting, 207–8

Creamed Spinach, 126

Creamy Coleslaw, 64

Dip
	Feta Dip, 122
	Guacamole, 56
	Hot Honey Cilantro Sauce, 112
	Melissa's Bean Dip, 58
	Roasted Salsa, 59
	Sriracha Lime Sauce, 112
	Vinegar Dipping Sauce, 75–76

Donut Holes, 172

Dressing
	Basil Balsamic Dressing, 25

Blue Cheese Vinaigrette, 27
Eggless Caesar Dressing, 26
Lemon Vinaigrette, 27
Mayonnaise, 24
Sesame Dressing, 25
Dry Rub Ribs, Indoor, 110
Dry Spice Rub, 16
Eggless Caesar Dressing, 26
Feta Dip, 122
Foccacia, Rosemary Sea Salt, 216
Granola, 94
Grilled Asparagus with Truffle Oil, 124
Guacamole, 56
Halibut with Couscous and Sundried
    Tomatoes, 168
Herb Butter, 72
Honey Chipotle Sauce, 20
Hot Honey Cilantro Sauce, 112
Indoor Dry Rub Ribs, 110
Jerk Spice Rub, 16
Kettle Corn, 170
Lemon
    Backyard Citrus Chicken, 132
    Buttercake Bakery Lemon Bars,
        134–36
    Citrus Almond Cake, 204–6
    Lemon Dijon Roasted Brussels
        Sprouts, 104
    Lemon Vinaigrette, 27
Linda's Chocolate Chip Cookie Pie,
    198–200
Marinade
    Asian Marinade, 21
    BBQ Sauce, 18
    Chimichurri Sauce, 20

Honey Chipotle Sauce, 20
Soy Balsamic Marinade, 21
Mashed Potatoes, 30
Mayonnaise, 24
Mediterranean Beef Stew, 156
Melissa's Bean Dip, 58
Mom's Chocolate Chip Toffee
    Cookies, 38
Mussels with Sausage, 158
Mustard Sauce, 154
Orange Currant Scones, Buttercake
    Bakery, 120–21
Oven-Baked Chicken Wings, 112
Panna Cotta, 140
Pecan Snowballs, Buttercake Bakery,
    201–2
Pesto
    Arugula Pesto, 62
    Sundried Tomato Pesto, 62
Pickles, Cora's Sliced Sweet, 150
Pulled Pork Sandwiches, 154
Pumpkin Whoopie Pies, Buttercake
    Bakery, 207–8
Quinoa Tabbouleh, 66–67
Raspberry Jalapeño Limeade, 86
Roasted Carrots, 102
Roasted Chickpeas, 96
Roasted Salsa, 59
Roasted Tomato Soup, 98
Rosemary Sea Salt Focaccia, 216
Rub
    Dry Spice Rub, 16
    Jerk Spice Rub, 16
Salad
    Cold Asian Peanut Noodle Salad,

    128
Cornbread Panzanella, 100
Tandoori Salmon Salad, 130
Sangria, Velvet Hammer, 142
Scallion Parmesan Drop Biscuits, 70
Seafood
    Halibut with Couscous and
        Sundried Tomatoes, 168
    Mussels with Sausage, 158
    Spicy Shrimp Tacos, 108
    Tandoori Salmon Salad, 130
Sesame Dressing, 25
Soy Balsamic Marinade, 21
Spicy Shrimp Tacos, 108
Sriracha-Honey Butter, 74
Sriracha Lime Sauce, 112
Sundried Tomatoes
    Blue Cheese Sundried Tomato
        Butter, 74
    Halibut with Couscous and
        Sundried Tomatoes, 168
    Sundried Tomato Basil Frittatas, 28
    Sundried Tomato Pesto, 62
Tandoori Salmon Salad, 130
Three-Pepper Jelly and Baked Brie, 68
Turkey
    Turkey Chili, 160–61
    Turkey Meatballs, 32
Vegetable Coconut Curry, 162
Veggie Fritters, 75–76
Velvet Hammer Sangria, 142
Vinegar Dipping Sauce, 75–76
Whole Roasted Chicken, 36
Wine-Braised Brisket, 166